CHIA
QUINOA
KALE
OH MY!

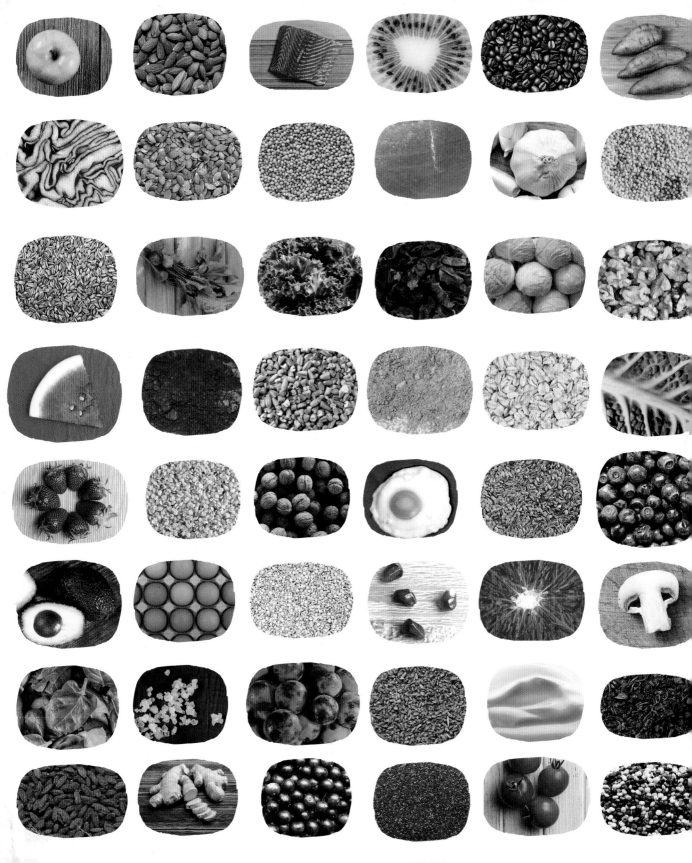

RECIPES FOR **40+** DELICIOUS,
SUPER-NUTRITIOUS
SUPERFOODS

CHIA QUINOA KALE

OH MY!

Cassie Johnston

THE COUNTRYMAN PRESS · WOODSTOCK, VT.

Published by The Countryman Press,
P.O. Box 748, Woodstock, VT 05091

Distributed by W. W. Norton & Company, Inc.,
500 Fifth Avenue, New York, NY 10110

Book Design by Natalie Olsen, Kisscut Design

Printed in The United States

Chia, Qunioa, Kale, Oh My!
ISBN 978-1-58157-274-2

10 9 8 7 6 5 4 3 2 1

CONTENTS

THE FOOD YOU EAT CAN BE
EITHER THE SAFEST AND MOST
POWERFUL FORM OF MEDICINE OR
THE SLOWEST FORM OF POISON.

—Ann Wigmore

Preface

I used to not put much thought into what I was eating. I had heard that veggies were good for me and that maybe I shouldn't eat so much fast food. But in my day-to-day life, I just didn't think it mattered that much. So I kept hitting up the drive-thru, scoffing at salads, and using speed dial to order from my favorite pizza place. After all, how bad could it be if I was still walking around feeling okay? I didn't have any major health problems. I was able to get out of bed in the morning. I felt *fine*. How much could my diet be affecting me if I couldn't feel it?

Over the years, as I gained more and more knowledge about nutrition, my food philosophy shifted. It wasn't overnight, but as I made more changes to what I put in my body, I started to notice that I actually had felt bad before—I just didn't know it. I had never known what "good" felt like and without that frame of reference, I'd thought my daily crash at 2 p.m., my acne-covered skin, and my brittle hair and nails were totally normal—when, in fact, they were signs of my body crying out for nourishing, healthy food. I thought I was fine, but I didn't realize how *un*fine I was until I started *actually* feeling good.

Now, I'm not immune to the appeal of a good slice (or two) of gooey, cheesy pizza, but I try to put those kinds of foods into my diet with a sense of balance. I want to keep feeling great, and that means including foods that nourish my body—not just fill my empty stomach and satisfy my taste buds.

As I became more and more interested in deeply nourishing foods, I started to learn more about the concept of superfoods—foods that are more nutrient-dense than other items on the grocery store shelves. I loved the idea that you could really, truly give your body what it craves nutritionally by focusing on a select group of superstar foods (many of which are readily available in most areas of North America). It really helped simplify healthy eating to me. Learning where to start when overhauling your diet can be incredibly overwhelming, but by focusing on packing your meals with a handful of superfoods that you and your family love to eat, you'll begin on solid footing.

This book is filled with over 100 recipes that spotlight some of my favorite superhero foods. I've tested (and tasted) each of these recipes in my very own home kitchen, and think I've come up with a collection of dishes that are not only super nourishing, but also super delicious. Just because they're packed with healthy ingredients, it doesn't mean all the recipes are low in calories, fat, or carbs—in fact, some of them are quite indulgent! What it does mean is that with each bite of these dishes, your body will thank you for giving it a hefty dose of the vitamins, minerals, and other nutrients it craves—even if that's in the form of ice cream.

Thank you for letting me into your kitchen!

♡ Cassy

Let's Talk Superfoods

We all know that the best way to nourish our bodies is to eat lots of fresh fruits and vegetables, whole grains, and lean proteins, but what if we could take a nutritious diet beyond just the standard finds at the grocery store? What if there were foods so nutritionally dense that they went above and beyond the regular definition of "healthy?" What if there were foods that have been proven to prevent cancer and reverse heart disease? What if there were foods whose health benefits were so powerful that they could be deemed *super?*

WHAT IF THERE WERE FOODS WHOSE HEALTH BENEFITS WERE SO POWERFUL THAT THEY COULD BE DEEMED SUPER?

Superfoods are just that—foods that are so nutritionally dense that they go above and beyond the regular definition of healthy. They aren't just foods that are low calorie, high in vitamins, or packed with fiber— they're foods that have been shown in study after study to make the human body healthier and stronger. They're foods that fight many of the common ailments that inflict our society today. They're foods that satisfy our hunger and satisfy our health.

While the term *superfoods* is thrown around to cover a large number of foods, there is no one definitive source on what is and isn't considered a superfood. In this cookbook, you'll find recipes for over 40 of the most commonly agreed-upon superfoods. And while every doctor, nutritionist, chef, and home cook may be able to list what they consider superpowerful foods, your list might not look anything like theirs (or the one found in this book). The best recommendation: Figure out what foods make you feel great and make you feel super— those are *your* personal superfoods.

About This Cookbook

In the pages of this book, you'll find over 100 recipes that spotlight some of the world's healthiest foods. When developing these recipes, I tried to make sure they were the cleanest, healthiest recipes I could make (while still keeping them super yummy!). Here are some things to keep in mind while cooking from this book.

Ingredients Matter

The truth is, a superfood is only as good as the other ingredients in the recipe. That's why you'll see lots of recipes in this book with superfood overlap and lots of clean, healthy ingredients that may not be standards in your kitchen (see Stock Your Superfood Kitchen, page 4).

Look Beyond Calories

Each of the recipes in this cookbook includes the basic nutritional information for a serving. While many folks value this information, I encourage you to look beyond the calories, fat, carbs, and protein numbers—they only tell part of the superfood story.

Just because a recipe is high in calories, it doesn't mean it should be a guilt-inducing dish. In fact, because many of the superfoods in this book are so nutritionally dense, you'll find that a lot of the higher-calorie recipes I include are the healthiest in terms of providing your body with the most nutrition. Not all calories are created equal! And the calories in this book are all good, healthy, nutritious calories that your body craves.

Raw Is (Often) Best

It's important to note that nutritionally speaking, many superfoods are at their best when eaten raw. Cooking can reduce (or even completely eliminate, in some rare cases) the powerful compounds that make super-foods so good for you. So, enjoy the cooked recipes in this book, but make sure you're also getting your fair share of raw, fresh foods, too!

Stock Your Superfood Kitchen

If you aren't a frequent customer to your local health food store, you'll probably notice a lot of oddball ingredients on the pages of this book. I promise it's not because I want to make your grocery bill skyrocket—it's because I want to make sure these recipes are as clean and healthy as possible, and that includes using the healthiest options available for their ingredients.

Following is a list of some of the pantry staples that will help you navigate the recipes in this book (as well as some more common substitutions, if you can't get your hands on the original ingredient).

INGREDIENT	DESCRIPTION	SUBSTITUTIONS
Cacao nibs	These little chunks of raw cacao are like the unprocessed cousin to chocolate chips. Unsweetened and richly chocolaty, they're a great way to add chocolate flavor!	Chocolate chips Chopped dark chocolate
Coconut oil	Often considered the healthiest cooking oil, coconut oil is packed with a unique combo of nutrient compounds that aren't found in other cooking oils.	Butter All other cooking oils
Fresh lemons and limes	You'll notice that many of the recipes in this book call for fresh lemon and lime juice and zest. It's a great way to impart tons of fresh flavor!	Bottled juice Vinegar
Greek yogurt	Thick and tangy Greek yogurt is a great high-nutrition substitute for mayo or sour cream in cooking and baking.	Mayonnaise Sour cream Regular yogurt
Medjool dates	One of the sweetest fruits on the planet, tender Medjool dates are available in most super-markets now.	Other dried fruit
Natural peanut butter	Many peanut butters you find on store shelves are packed with additives and sugar. Try to find a peanut butter that is just peanuts and salt.	Regular peanut butter Almond butter Sunflower butter

INGREDIENT	DESCRIPTION	SUBSTITUTIONS
Olive oil	Almost every home cook has a vial of olive oil in the pantry. In this book, you'll see it listed in two different ways. Pick up a high-quality extra-virgin olive oil for when the oil is used raw, and you can stick to a regular organic olive oil when the oil is used for cooking.	All other cooking oils
Organic cane sugar	This is the less-processed version of regular table sugar. It's a good option for baked goods but, like all sweeteners, should be eaten in moderation.	Turbinado sugar Raw sugar Table sugar Coconut sugar Maple sugar Sucanat
Pure maple syrup	Not just for pancakes, pure maple syrup is an all-natural, vegan sweetener that is a great option for all-purpose sweetening.	Honey Agave nectar Cane juice
Sea salt	Not all salt is created equal! All-natural sea salt is packed with minerals.	Table salt Kosher salt
Unfiltered cider vinegar	The health benefits of unfiltered cider vinegar could fill their own book! Look for organic, unfiltered vinegar for the best health benefits and flavor.	All other vinegars Lemon or lime juice
Unsweetened applesauce	Aside from being yummy, unsweetened applesauce is a workhorse of a superfood kitchen! Use it to sweeten smoothies and moisten baked goods.	Pumpkin puree
Unsweetened shredded coconut	Coconut has a natural sweetness that really comes out when it's dehydrated and shredded.	None
White whole wheat flour	White whole wheat flour is a whole-grain flour made from soft white wheat, giving it a milder flavor than your typical whole wheat flour.	Whole wheat flour All-purpose flour
Whole wheat panko	Panko bread crumbs are a great way to make a crunchy breading or use as a filler. Try to track down whole wheat panko for the highest nutrition.	Regular panko Regular bread crumbs Smashed saltines

1

BREAKFAST

9   19   51   60

TROPICAL ZINGER AÇAI BOWL

Never heard of an açai bowl? No worries, you aren't alone.
Even though açai bowls are so popular in Brazil as to be served
at beachside kiosks, they're a newcomer to North America.
Basically, an açai bowl is a frosty, creamy bowl of açai berry puree
mixed with other fruits and topped with your favorite toppings—
it's like eating a superhealthy ice cream sundae for breakfast!

MAKES: *1 serving*
TIME: *5 minutes*

For the puree

1 cup frozen açai berry puree
(see note about availability on page 10)

½ ripe banana, frozen

¼ cup coconut milk

¼ cup fresh pineapple chunks

1 teaspoon grated fresh ginger

For the toppings

½ ripe banana, sliced

¼ cup granola

⅓ cup unsweetened shredded coconut

To prepare the puree, in a blender, combine all the puree ingredients. Blend on high speed until very smooth.

Pour into a bowl and sprinkle with the toppings.

NUTRITION PER SERVING: 452 CALORIES, 18.3 G FAT, 67.9 G CARBS, 6.4 G PROTEIN

LEARN MORE ABOUT WHY GINGER IS A GREAT ADDITION TO YOUR DIET ON PAGE 163.

AÇAI BERRIES

Unless you live in the Amazon, you might not have had much exposure to the dark purple açai berry (pronounced "aah-sai-ee"). Thankfully for those of us not in the jungle, açai products have made their way to supermarket shelves in recent years due to the berry's explosive flavor and extraordinary nutrition profile.

QUICK FACTS

❶ This fruit contains one of the highest amounts of antioxidants among any food on the planet.
❷ Açai berries are a great source of healthy fats.
❸ The unique combination of amino acids, fatty acids, and antioxidants in açai berries may help slow the aging process.

HEALTH BENEFITS

Many research studies have shown that açai berries are one of the highest-known sources for antioxidants—higher than other antioxidant powerhouses such as blueberries and strawberries. In Brazil, açai berries are nicknamed "the beauty berry" because they have numerous benefits to the condition of the skin, hair, and body. Some even think a diet rich in açai will help slow the aging process!

AVAILABILITY

It's nearly impossible to find fresh açai berries in North American supermarkets, but don't worry, there are numerous açai products on the shelves that will still get you the benefits of the berries. Look for 100 percent pure açai berry puree in the frozen fruit section of your local health food store. You can also look for 100 percent pure açai berry juice, usually located in the produce section of your supermarket. Just make sure to avoid açai products that are loaded with added sugar or flavors—you want to look for products that list açai as the first ingredient.

HOW TO USE

You can use the puree and juice in smoothies and baking for a tasty burst of tropical flavor! If you manage to get your hands on some fresh açai berries, eat them just as you would any other berry. And just like other berries, keep in mind that cooking begins to deteriorate the powerful compounds in the açai berry, so make sure to get your fill of raw or lightly cooked berries.

NUTRITION HIGHLIGHTS PER 1 CUP AÇAI BERRIES

284	6g	31g	1g	30%	24%	16%
CALORIES	FAT	CARBS	PROTEIN	VITAMIN A	DIETARY FIBER	VITAMIN C

SPINACH

We've all heard that we need to get a good dose of dark, leafy greens every week, and spinach is a great, mild-flavored way to hit your quota. Spinach is missing the earthy flavor that a lot of dark, leafy greens possess, making it a great way to add nutrients to all kinds of dishes without overpowering the flavor.

QUICK FACTS

1 Spinach is one of the most nutritionally dense foods on the planet, containing over 25 percent of your RDA of many vitamins and minerals.

2 Spinach contains a unique combination of nutrients that helps support bone health.

3 Try to get organic spinach whenever possible, as nonorganic spinach is grown using high levels of pesticides.

HEALTH BENEFITS

Spinach is one of the most nutritionally dense foods on the planet, containing more than 25 percent of your recommended daily allowance of 10 vitamins and minerals in just one serving. Spinach is particularly dense in vitamin K, an important nutrient that helps maintain bone health. Combined with decent amounts of other bone-supporting nutrients, such as calcium and magnesium, spinach is a veggie that'll help make you big and strong!

And while almost all the foods in this book contain phytonutrients, spinach in particular has a unique combination of more than a dozen compounds that have particularly strong function as anticancer compounds.

AVAILABILITY

You can find both fresh and frozen spinach on the shelves of most grocery stores, but if possible, try to buy organic. Conventionally grown spinach is considered one of the "dirtiest" veggies in the produce section— some reports state that nearly 50 different chemicals and pesticides can be found on the leaves of nonorganic spinach.

HOW TO USE

Spinach's mild flavor and delicate texture make it a great option for adding some nutrients into almost any dish. Throw a handful into your favorite pasta sauce, puree it and put it into brownies, or toss some into your favorite smoothie combination.

NUTRITION HIGHLIGHTS PER 1 CUP RAW SPINACH

7	0.1g	1.1g	0.9g	987%	105%	84%
CALORIES	FAT	CARBS	PROTEIN	VITAMIN B12	VITAMIN A	MANGANESE

APPLE PIE SPINACH SMOOTHIE

Dessert for breakfast? Sure! This smoothie tastes just like a slice of classic apple pie, but it's healthy enough to make a balanced breakfast. Don't be afraid of the green color! The deep flavor of apples and cinnamon mask all the earthiness of the spinach.

MAKES: 1 serving
TIME: 5 minutes

½ cup milk

½ cup apple juice

½ cup unsweetened applesauce

1 cup fresh spinach

½ cup plain Greek yogurt

1 banana

Pinch of ground cinnamon

A few ice cubes

Blend all the ingredients in a blender on high speed until very smooth.

NUTRITION PER SERVING: 325 CALORIES, 2 G FAT, 66 G CARBS, 15 G PROTEIN

TWEAK THE SPICES TO SUIT YOUR TASTES. GROUND GINGER, CLOVES, AND NUTMEG ARE ALL GREAT ADDITIONS!

WHOLE WHEAT APPLE RAISIN BREAD

Quick breads are a great way to get started with bread making if you're a little intimidated. No worries about activated yeast or rising times—you just mix up the batter, let it bake, and you've got tender, sliceable, yummy fruit bread. This lightly sweet bread is a perfect option for breakfast. I like to serve it with a small spread of butter and a big cup of coffee.

MAKES: *12 slices*
TIME: *1 hour 15 minutes*

¼ cup melted coconut oil

4 tablespoons butter, melted

½ cup packed brown sugar

¼ cup pure maple syrup

1 cup unsweetened applesauce

2 large eggs

1 teaspoon baking soda

½ teaspoon baking powder

½ teaspoon salt

1 teaspoon ground cinnamon

¼ teaspoon ground nutmeg

2 ¼ cups white whole wheat flour

1 cup raisins

1 medium-size apple, cored and diced

½ cup chopped pecans

Preheat the oven to 350°F. In a large mixing bowl, whisk together the coconut oil, butter, brown sugar, maple syrup, applesauce, and eggs. Set aside. In a medium-size mixing bowl, sift together the baking soda, baking powder, salt, cinnamon, nutmeg, and flour. Add the dry ingredients to the wet, stirring until just combined; do not overmix. Fold in the raisins, apple, and pecans. Spoon the batter into a parchment-lined 8 1/2 x 4 1/2-inch loaf pan. Bake for 50 to 60 minutes, or until the top is browned and begins to crack, and a toothpick inserted into the center comes out clean. Let cool completely in the pan before slicing.

NUTRITION PER SERVING: 253 CALORIES, 9.7 G FAT, 40.4 G CARBS, 4.4 G PROTEIN

FEEL FREE TO PLAY WITH THE
MIX-INS. LEAVE OUT THE NUTS,
ADD SOME CHOCOLATE CHIPS,
OR EVEN SWAP IN ANOTHER
DRIED FRUIT FOR THE RAISINS.

CHOCO-CHIA-CHERRY SMOOTHIE

The pairing of chocolate and cherry is one of my favorite flavor combinations. This superhealthy smoothie also happens to be superdecadent and rich!

MAKES: *2 servings*
TIME: *5 minutes*

1 cup unsweetened nut, soy, or cow's milk

2 tablespoons chia seeds

1 tablespoon unsweetened cocoa powder

2 cups pitted, halved cherries

1 medium-size ripe banana

4 to 5 ice cubes

Combine all the ingredients in the order listed in a blender. Blend on high speed until everything is smooth. Pour into two glasses (or one big glass!) and serve.

NUTRITION PER SERVING: 217 CALORIES, 7.1 G FAT, 40.6 G CARBS, 5.8 G PROTEIN

IF YOUR BANANA ISN'T VERY RIPE, YOU MIGHT WANT TO ADD A TOUCH OF PURE MAPLE SYRUP OR HONEY TO SWEETEN THE SMOOTHIE.

LEMON CHIA MUFFINS

So often, *muffin* is just a code word for *cake*. But these lemon-scented, whole-grain muffins are lightly sweet and perfect for eating at the breakfast table or on the go.

MAKES: 24 muffins
TIME: 40 minutes

3 cups white whole wheat flour

1 teaspoon baking powder

½ teaspoon baking soda

½ teaspoon salt

1 cup cane sugar

½ cup melted coconut oil

½ cup unsweetened applesauce

2 large eggs

1 cup plain Greek yogurt

Zest and juice of 2 lemons

¼ cup chia seeds

Preheat the oven to 350°F. Place 24 paper baking cups in the cups of a muffin tin; set aside. In a large bowl, sift together the flour, baking powder, baking soda, salt, and cane sugar. In a small bowl, whisk together the coconut oil, applesauce, eggs, Greek yogurt, lemon juice and zest, and chia seeds. Pour the wet ingredients into the dry, and stir together until just combined. It will be a very thick batter; do not overmix. Spoon the batter into the prepared muffin tin until the cups are two-thirds full. Bake for 20 to 25 minutes, or until the tops are lightly browned and a toothpick inserted into the center of a muffin comes out clean.

NUTRITION PER SERVING: 140 CALORIES, 5.6 G FAT, 20.8 G CARBS, 3.7 G PROTEIN

FOR AN ADDED SUPERFOOD TREAT, FOLD IN 2 CUPS OF FRESH BLUEBERRIES RIGHT BEFORE BAKING.

DARK CHOCOLATE, PISTACHIO & ORANGE YOGURT PARFAIT

Chocolate isn't just for dessert anymore! This yogurt parfait is a not-too-sweet way to get in a bit of chocolate for breakfast or a snack—plus, you get tons of healthy fats and protein from the Greek yogurt.

MAKES: 1 serving
TIME: 5 minutes

1 cup plain Greek yogurt

¼ cup chopped pistachios

2 tablespoons chopped dark chocolate

1 tablespoon honey

Zest of 1 orange

In a small cup, top ½ cup of the yogurt with half of the pistachios, chocolate, honey, and orange zest. Top with the remaining Greek yogurt, pistachios, chocolate, honey, and orange zest.

NUTRITION PER SERVING: 454 CALORIES, 20.5 G FAT, 45.7 G CARBS, 26.3 G PROTEIN

I LIKE TO PACK THESE IN SMALL CANNING JARS AND TAKE THEM ON THE GO.

BAKED ASPARAGUS & EGGS

This quick-together meal is a dish that knows no time restraints. Eat it for breakfast, brunch, lunch, dinner, or even a midnight snack, and you'll be satisfied!

MAKES: *2 servings*
TIME: *15 minutes*

2 tablespoons butter

Pinch of red pepper flakes

2 cloves garlic, minced

1 medium-size onion, diced

1 pound asparagus, ends trimmed, cut into 1-inch pieces

4 large eggs

Salt and pepper

Juice of ½ lemon

Preheat the broiler to high. Put the butter in a medium-size cast-iron or other ovenproof skillet. Place the skillet under the broiler to melt the butter. Once the butter is melted, add the red pepper flakes, garlic, onion, and asparagus. Place back under the broiler and cook for about 5 minutes, or until the asparagus is tender but not fully cooked. Push aside the asparagus mixture to make space and crack the eggs into the skillet. Place back under the broiler and cook for 2 to 3 minutes, or until the whites are cooked through but the yolks are still soft. Remove from the broiler, top with salt and pepper to taste, and the lemon juice. Serve directly from the skillet with crusty bread or divide into individual plates to serve.

NUTRITION PER SERVING: 298 CALORIES, 20.0 G FAT, 16 G CARBS, 17 G PROTEIN

THE SOFT-COOKED EGGS
CREATE A SILKY SAUCE
FOR THE ASPARAGUS,
BUT IF YOU'RE AVOIDING
RAW EGG YOLK, JUST COOK
THE EGGS A BIT LONGER
TO SET THE YOLK.

THE METHOD
FOR THESE CUPS
IS INFINITELY
ADAPTABLE.
TRY A VERSION
WITH HAM,
CHEDDAR CHEESE,
AND SLICED
GREEN ONIONS,
TOO!

HERBED EGG, TURKEY & GOAT CHEESE CUPS

These handheld cups make a perfect on-the-go breakfast for busy families. I like to make up a batch of these on the weekend and then stash them in the fridge for hectic mornings throughout the week.

MAKES: *8 servings*
TIME: *10 minutes*

Cooking spray

½ teaspoon dried parsley

½ teaspoon dried dill

½ teaspoon dried thyme

½ teaspoon dried rosemary

½ teaspoon kosher salt

½ teaspoon ground black pepper

8 slices roasted turkey breast

8 large eggs

2 ounces goat cheese

Preheat the oven to 425°F. Spray eight cups of a muffin tin with cooking spray; set aside. In a small bowl, combine the parsley, dill, thyme, rosemary, salt, and pepper; set aside. Press a slice of turkey into each of the greased muffin cups. Gently break an egg into each slice of turkey. Crumble the goat cheese evenly among each of the eight cups. Sprinkle the top of each muffin cup with the herb mixture, dividing evenly. Bake until the eggs reach your desired doneness: 10 minutes for runny yolks, 12 minutes for soft yolks, and 14 minutes for hard-cooked yolks.

NUTRITION PER SERVING: 111 CALORIES, 7.3 G FAT, 1.0 G CARBS, 9.9 G PROTEIN

MANGO, BANANA & FLAX SMOOTHIE

This tropical smoothie will help you feel as if you're relaxing on a beach (even if you're stuck inside at home), and a heavy dose of ground flaxseeds gives it a nice boost of protein, fat, and omega-3s.

MAKES: *2 servings*
TIME: *5 minutes*

1 ripe mango, peeled, pitted, and chopped roughly

1 large ripe banana

2 tablespoons ground flaxseeds

½ cup plain Greek yogurt

1 cup milk

Handful of ice cubes

IF IT'S TOASTY OUTSIDE, THIS SMOOTHIE ALSO MAKES FOR GREAT POPSICLES. JUST LEAVE OUT THE ICE CUBES, AND POUR IT INTO A POPSICLE MOLD AND FREEZE.

Blend all the ingredients in a blender on high speed until very smooth. Pour into two glasses and serve immediately.

NUTRITION PER SERVING: 267 CALORIES, 4.9 G FAT, 43.1 G CARBS, 13.2 G PROTEIN

IMMUNE-BOOSTING GINGER TEA

Sipping on a steaming mug of tea when you're feeling under the weather is nothing new, but this brew can actually help you kick your cold. Ginger, lemon, and honey are three of the best natural remedies for boosting your immune system. Make sure to drink this all-natural tea frequently to keep your immune system strong!

MAKES: 1 serving
TIME: 10 minutes

6 thin slices peeled ginger

Juice of ½ lemon

1 tablespoon honey

1 ½ cups boiling water

Combine the ginger, lemon, and honey in a large mug. Pour in the boiling water, and allow to steep for 10 minutes.

NUTRITION PER SERVING: 71 CALORIES, 0.1 G FAT, 18.7 G CARBS, 0.2 G PROTEIN

THE LONGER YOU STEEP THIS TEA, THE STRONGER AND SPICIER THE GINGER GETS.

GINGER CARROT JUICE ZINGER

This tangy juice isn't for the faint of heart, but if you feel a cold coming on, this just might be the tonic that stops that yucky virus in its tracks. It's packed with immune-boosting goodies, and the cool juice feels great on a scratchy throat.

MAKES: 1 serving
TIME: 5 minutes

5 carrots

1 (½-inch) piece of fresh ginger, peeled

½ lemon

1 cucumber

1 grapefruit, peeled and seeded

1 apple, cored

Process all the ingredients through a juicer. Stir the juice to mix. Enjoy at room temperature, or chill and enjoy cold.

NUTRITION PER TABLESPOON: 162 CALORIES, 1.0 G FAT, 48.9 G CARBS, 4.4 G PROTEIN

IF THIS MIXTURE IS A BIT TOO TART FOR YOUR TASTE, THROW IN ANOTHER APPLE, OR ONLY USE HALF OF A GRAPEFRUIT.

GOJI BERRY & GINGER YOGURT SCONES

The key to keeping these scones light and fluffy is all in the flour. White whole wheat flour is a staple in my kitchen because it's a 100 percent whole-grain flour, but it results in light and tender baked goods that are similar in texture and taste to those made with all-purpose flour. How do they do it? Well, white whole wheat flour is ground from a different variety of wheat berries than your typical whole wheat flour. These wheat berries are milder and softer, resulting in a mild-tasting, soft flour.

MAKES: 6 scones
TIME: 35 minutes

2 cups white whole wheat flour

2 tablespoons cane sugar, plus extra for garnish

2 teaspoons baking powder

1 teaspoon baking soda

¼ teaspoon salt

½ cup (1 stick, 4 ounces) butter, cut into small pieces and frozen

¾ cup plain, low-fat Greek yogurt

1 large egg

1 tablespoon fresh ground ginger

½ cup dried goji berries

1 large egg white

IF YOU CAN'T FIND WHITE WHOLE WHEAT FLOUR, YOU CAN ALSO SUB IN HALF REGULAR WHOLE WHEAT FLOUR AND HALF ALL-PURPOSE FLOUR.

Preheat the oven to 375°F. Line a baking sheet with a piece of parchment paper; set aside. In a food processor, combine the flour, sugar, baking powder, baking soda, and salt. Pulse until combined. Add the butter, and pulse until the butter pieces are about the size of peas, or slightly smaller. Transfer the mixture to a large mixing bowl. Add the yogurt, egg, ginger, and goji berries. Using a wooden spoon or clean hands, mix the dough until it just comes together. The dough will be rough and slightly dry—do not overmix! Place the dough on a clean surface and form into a disk about 10 inches in diameter and 1 inch thick. Using a sharp knife, cut the disk into six equal pie-shaped wedges. Transfer the scones to the prepared baking sheet. Using a pastry brush, brush each scone lightly with egg white, then sprinkle with cane sugar. Bake for 17 to 20 minutes, or until golden brown.

NUTRITION PER SCONE: 343 CALORIES, 17.8 G FAT, 38.4 G CARBS, 10.2 G PROTEIN

GRAPE POWER JUICE

Vegetable juice is a great way to get a ton of healthy vitamins and minerals without having to eat a truckload of produce. But there's one problem. Vegetable juice often tastes like . . . vegetables. That's no fun. This juice recipe not only gets you the awesome benefits of juicing veggies and healthy fruits, but it also tastes amazing! It's sweet, tangy, and smooth. This is a great vegetable juice for newbies to juicing.

MAKES: 1 serving
TIME: 5 minutes

2 stalks celery

½ cucumber

1 cup baby spinach

2 carrots

1 apple, cored

2 cups red grapes

¼ lemon

Process all the ingredients through a juicer. Stir the juice to mix. Enjoy at room temperature, or chill and enjoy cold.

NUTRITION PER SERVING: 135 CALORIES, 1.26 G FAT, 42.2 G CARBS, 3.8 G PROTEIN

IF YOU'RE GOING TO SPRING FOR ORGANIC PRODUCE, JUICING IS THE TIME TO DO SO. BECAUSE YOU'RE USING THE PEELS, YOU'LL WANT THEM TO BE CHEMICAL FREE. IF YOU WANT TO USE CONVENTIONAL FRUITS AND VEGGIES, JUST MAKE SURE TO PEEL THEM BEFORE JUICING.

BUTTERNUT SQUASH & KALE HASH

Bacon has a bad rap when it comes to healthy eating, but the truth is, just as long as you don't overdo it, good-quality bacon is a great way to add a ton of flavor to a dish without adding a ton of calories. For the healthiest bacon, keep an eye out for nitrate-free brands that are naturally flavored.

MAKES: 4 servings
TIME: 20 minutes

2 slices thick-cut bacon

1 small butternut squash, peeled, seeded, and diced (about 2 pounds)

2 cloves garlic, minced

½ large onion, diced

1 bunch kale, torn into bite-size pieces (about 6 leaves)

Salt and pepper

Cook the bacon in a large skillet over medium-high heat until crisp. Remove from the pan, crumble, and set aside. Add the squash to the bacon grease in the skillet and cook until the squash begins to brown and soften, about 5 minutes. Add the garlic and onion and continue to cook until the onion is soft and the squash is fork tender. Add the kale, cover the pan, and let the kale wilt for 5 minutes. Season with salt and pepper to taste.

NUTRITION PER SERVING: 189 CALORIES, 4.2 G FAT, 34.0 G CARBS, 7.8 G PROTEIN

WE TOP THIS WITH A SUNNY-SIDE-UP EGG AND EAT IT FOR DINNER AT LEAST ONCE A WEEK.

COCONUT-PISTACHIO MILLET PORRIDGE

When finely ground, cooked millet has a silky, creamy texture that reminds me a lot of the cream of wheat I ate as a kid. I mixed ground millet in this porridge with shredded coconut to create a flavorful, whole-grain, gluten-free breakfast that'll leave you satisfied for hours.

MAKES: 1 serving
TIME: 15 minutes

⅔ cup coconut milk

⅔ cup water

1 tablespoon honey

Pinch of salt

⅓ cup millet, ground in a coffee grinder

¼ cup unsweetened shredded coconut

½ teaspoon vanilla extract

2 tablespoons chopped pistachios

In a small saucepan over medium-high heat, bring the coconut milk, water, honey, and salt to a boil. Whisk in the millet and coconut until there are no remaining lumps. Bring back to a boil, lower the heat, and simmer until the porridge is thick and creamy, about 10 minutes. Remove from the heat, stir in the vanilla, and top with chopped pistachios.

NUTRITION PER SERVING: 474 CALORIES, 16.1 G FAT, 70.5 G CARBS, 9.1 G PROTEIN

MILLET HAS A LIGHTLY SWEET FLAVOR ON ITS OWN, SO IT DOESN'T REQUIRE MUCH SWEETENER.

APPLE-DATE STEEL-CUT OATMEAL

Steel-cut oats take a lot longer to cook than the oats you're used to. To streamline this process, you can set up these oats in a slow cooker or rice cooker the night before, for a quick and easy breakfast in the morning.

MAKES: *4 servings*
TIME: *40 minutes*

1 cup steel-cut oats

3 cups water

1 large tart apple, such as Granny Smith, cored and diced

6 Medjool dates, pitted and diced

½ teaspoon ground cinnamon

1 teaspoon vanilla extract

Pinch of kosher salt

In a saucepan, combine all the ingredients, bring to a boil over high heat, lower the heat, and simmer, stirring frequently, until all water is absorbed and the oats are tender—about 30 minutes. You may need to add more water to achieve your desired level of tenderness. Serve topped with milk, cream, maple syrup, butter, brown sugar, nuts, or other toppings, as desired.

NUTRITION PER SERVING: 290 CALORIES, 1.3 G FAT, 83.4 G CARBS, 4.2 G PROTEIN

THE DATES AND APPLES GO A LONG WAY TO SWEETEN THIS OATMEAL; TASTE IT BEFORE YOU ADD ANY SWEETENER!

OATMEAL-RAISIN BREAKFAST COOKIES

Cookies for breakfast? Absolutely! These whole-grain, lightly sweet cookies are a great way to kick off your day right. If you're pressed for time on most mornings, make up a big batch of these on a slow weekend and freeze. A few seconds in the microwave, and they're just like fresh baked!

MAKES: 18 cookies
TIME: 25 minutes

½ cup melted coconut oil

2 large eggs

1 teaspoon vanilla extract

½ cup unsweetened applesauce

¼ cup honey

1 ½ cups whole wheat flour

1 cup rolled oats

¼ cup ground flaxseeds

½ teaspoon baking soda

½ teaspoon ground cinnamon

½ cup raisins

THE UNSWEETENED APPLESAUCE AND TOUCH OF HONEY MAKES THESE COOKIES LIGHTLY SWEET— PERFECT FOR BREAKFAST.

Preheat the oven to 350°F. Line a baking sheet with parchment paper; set aside. In a small bowl, whisk together the coconut oil, eggs, vanilla, applesauce, and honey until well combined. In a medium-size mixing bowl, stir together the flour, oats, ground flaxseeds, baking soda, cinnamon, and raisins until well combined. Add the wet ingredients and stir until completely mixed. The batter will be wet. Allow the batter to rest for 5 minutes (this helps thicken it a bit). Spoon rounded tablespoons, 2 inches apart, onto the prepared baking sheet. Bake for 12 to 15 minutes, or until the cookies are golden brown around the edges. Let cool for 5 minutes on the baking sheet, then transfer to cooling rack to cool completely.

NUTRITION PER COOKIE: 153 CALORIES, 7.4 G FAT, 19.4 G CARBS, 2.7 G PROTEIN

SAVORY OATS
with Sunny-Side Egg

If the thought of savory oatmeal sounds weird to you, you'll just have to trust me on this one! It's an awesome change of pace from the normally sweet hot breakfast cereal. This is so yummy, you can eat it for breakfast, lunch, or a quick and easy weeknight dinner.

MAKES: 1 serving
TIME: 10 minutes

1 cup chicken or vegetable broth

¾ cup rolled oats

Pinch of salt and pepper

1 large egg

2 tablespoons shredded Cheddar cheese

1 tablespoon diced chives

Juice of ½ lemon

In a medium-size saucepan, combine the broth, oats, salt, and pepper. Bring to a boil over medium-high heat, lower the heat, and simmer for about 5 minutes, or until the oats have absorbed most of the liquid. Meanwhile, heat a small, nonstick skillet over medium-high heat. Crack in the egg and cook until the white is solid but the yolk is still runny, about 3 minutes. To serve, spoon the oats into a bowl and top with the Cheddar, chives, and egg. Squeeze lemon juice on top.

NUTRITION PER SERVING: 392 CALORIES, 14.4 G FAT, 43.2 G CARBS, 22.1 G PROTEIN

FEEL FREE TO PLAY WITH ADD-INS. BACON, CRUMBLED FETA CHEESE, AND SLICED GREEN ONIONS WOULD ALL BE AWESOME ADDITIONS!

OATS

If all you can think of when you think of oats is a big vat of gray, goopy slop served at breakfast buffets, then you're seriously missing out on their flavor and nutrition. The versatility of oats goes way beyond just oatmeal!

QUICK FACTS

1 Oats are one of the best foods you can eat for heart health.

2 A particular type of fiber in oats helps lower cholesterol and protect against cardiovascular disease.

3 Oats contain compounds that help regulate blood sugar and reduce the risk of type 2 diabetes.

4 Oats can be a good gluten-free option for people with gluten intolerances or celiac disease.

HEALTH BENEFITS

The specific type of fiber and antioxidants in oats seems to have a big impact on cholesterol. In particular, it seems the benefits of a diet rich in oats are important for the heart health of postmenopausal women.

The same type of fiber in oats that is healthy for the heart has been shown to stabilize the peaks and valleys of the blood sugar and help lower the risk of type 2 diabetes.

AVAILABILITY

At the grocery store, oats are available in a number of different levels of processing. Look for old-fashioned, rolled, steel-cut, or groats to get the most whole-grain benefit from your morning bowl of oatmeal. These options take a bit longer to cook than the highly processed quick-cook oats, but the health benefits are worth the extra time investment.

HOW TO USE

Depending on the cut of the oatmeal, the cooking time required might be anywhere from 5 to 50 minutes. But usually, a cooking ratio of two parts liquid to one part oats will create a satisfying breakfast porridge.

Uncooked oats can also be used as an add-in to granola bars, baked goods, and even a thickener when making burgers or meat loaf.

NUTRITION HIGHLIGHTS PER 1 CUP COOKED OATS

158   3.2g   27g   6g   96%   30%   27%

POMEGRANATES

It's only in recent years that the pomegranates have moved away from being a specialty food and earned a spot in many household fruit bowls—especially when they are in season during fall and winter. Their superfood status might have something to do with the increase in popularity. These strange-looking fruits have enough health benefits that it's worth tracking down a few.

QUICK FACTS

1. Pomegranates contain a special combination of antioxidants that help regulate blood pressure and prevent cancers.
2. Pomegranates are in season during fall and early winter.
3. Pure, unsweetened pomegranate juice is a great alternative to the fresh fruit.

HEALTH BENEFITS

Both the arils (seed sacs) of pomegranates and pomegranate juice are great options for enjoying the vitamin C, potassium, and antioxidant benefits of this fruit. Pomegranates contain a special combination of three antioxidants—tannins, anthocyanins, and ellagic acid—which are in particularly high doses in pomegranate juice. This combination of antioxidants has been shown to help prevent strokes and heart attacks by lowering blood pressure and reducing plaque in arteries. Pomegranates are also especially revered for the promising studies that show a diet rich in pomegranate may help prevent breast cancer, prostate cancer, colon cancer, and leukemia.

AVAILABILITY

Pomegranates are still hard to come by out of season, but if you look in the fall and early winter, you'll be able to find them in many larger supermarkets. Pure pomegranate juice is usually available year-round in the refrigerated juice section (and gets you the same health benefits as the fresh fruit).

HOW TO USE

If you've never approached a pomegranate before, you might be confused upon first cutting into one. The fruit has a red, tough exterior, and the interior is filled with white, inedible flesh and hundreds of red juice sacs (called arils) surrounding seeds. The arils are what you eat (and what makes the juice). Most folks just pull out the arils and use them whole, with their seed, for a crunchy, tangy topping to cereal, yogurt, or desserts.

RILS

.3 mg

SIUM

ORANGE-POMEGRANATE STEEL-CUT OATMEAL

If you've never cooked up a batch of steel-cut oats before, I highly recommend you get your hands on some and try it out. Nutty, chewy, and earthy—it's a totally different experience from your standard oatmeal. In fact, a lot of folks who think regular oatmeal is pasty and goopy actually love the texture of steel-cut oats. Plus, because steel-cut oats are so minimally processed, the nutritional benefits are quite impressive!

MAKES: 4 servings
TIME: 45 minutes

2 cups low-fat milk

1 ½ cups water

Juice and zest of 1 orange

Pinch of salt

1 cup steel-cut oats

¼ cup pure maple syrup

½ cup pomegranate arils

¼ cup hulled sunflower seeds

Bring the milk, water, orange juice and zest, and salt to a boil in a medium-size saucepan over medium-high heat. Once boiling, stir in the oats, lower the heat, and simmer for 30 to 40 minutes, or until the oatmeal is thick and no longer liquidy. Divide among four bowls and serve topped with the maple syrup, pomegranate arils, and sunflower seeds.

NUTRITION PER SERVING: 274 CALORIES, 8.9 G FAT, 40.8 G CARBS, 10.0 G PROTEIN

STEEL-CUT OATS TAKE LONGER TO COOK THAN ROLLED OR INSTANT OATS, SO MAKE SURE YOU HAVE A LEISURELY MORNING TO DEVOTE TO THIS RECIPE.

POM-BERRY SMOOTHIE

Want to kick off your morning with a double dose of antioxidants? If so, then you need to whip up one of these smoothies. Not only will your body thank you for the nutrients from the pomegranates, but it'll also be super grateful for a good dose of cancer-fighting berries. Your taste buds will be pretty happy, too.

MAKES: *2 (8-ounce) servings*
TIME: *10 minutes*

½ cup pomegranate juice

1 cup frozen mixed berries

½ cup plain, low-fat Greek yogurt

1 tablespoon honey

Blend all the ingredients in a blender on high speed until very smooth. Pour into two glasses and serve immediately.

NUTRITION PER SERVING: 153 CALORIES, 1.3 G FAT, 28.7 G CARBS, 6.2 G PROTEIN

YOU CAN EASILY SUB IN FRESH BERRIES FOR FROZEN IN THIS RECIPE; JUST TOSS IN A HANDFUL OF ICE CUBES TO MAKE THE SMOOTHIE ICY.

PUMPKIN SPICE GRANOLA

This granola fills your entire house with an amazing, warm, autumnal scent that alone makes it worth whipping up. And that's not taking into account how totally delicious it is! Serve this up atop your favorite yogurt for an awesome seasonal breakfast.

MAKES: 7 cups
TIME: 45 minutes

4 cups rolled oats

1 ½ cups hulled pumpkin seeds

1 cup halved pecans

¼ cup ground flaxseeds

¼ cup chia seeds

½ cup pure pumpkin puree

⅓ cup pure maple syrup

2 tablespoons coconut oil, melted

1 tablespoon vanilla extract

1 tablespoon ground cinnamon

½ teaspoon ground nutmeg

¼ teaspoon ground cloves

½ teaspoon salt

Preheat the oven to 325°F. In a large mixing bowl, combine the oats, pumpkin seeds, pecans, flaxseeds, and chia seeds. In a small bowl, whisk together the pumpkin puree, maple syrup, coconut oil, vanilla, cinnamon, nutmeg, cloves, and salt until smooth. Pour over the oat mixture. Toss until the oat mixture is well coated. Spread the mixture onto an ungreased baking sheet. Bake for 25 to 35 minutes, stirring every 10 minutes, or until browned and crunchy.

NUTRITION PER ½ CUP: 338 CALORIES, 22.6 G FAT, 27.8 G CARBS, 9.7 G PROTEIN

IF YOU LIKE BIGGER CHUNKS OF GRANOLA, STIR LESS FREQUENTLY WHILE IT'S BAKING.

FLAXSEEDS

Some experts consider flaxseed to be one of the most powerful food sources on the planet. That might be why you've seen a boom in flaxseed products on store shelves recently. Flax has been eaten since at least the eighth century, when King Charlemagne thought that the nutrients in flax were so important that he passed laws requiring his citizens to consume the seed regularly. Now that's a powerful superfood!

QUICK FACTS

❶ The unique structure of fatty acids in flax stands up well to cooking and baking.

❷ Flax is one of the highest known plant-based sources of omega-3 fatty acids.

❸ Ground flaxseed meal is easiest to digest and offers the most health benefits, but can become rancid if not stored properly.

❹ The high levels of antioxidant and anti-inflammatory compounds in flax benefit nearly every system in the body.

HEALTH BENEFITS

Like their superfood seed friend the chia seed, flaxseeds are packed with omega-3 fatty acids. The particular kind of fatty acid found in flax is even stable when heat is applied, making flax an awesome addition to baked goods.

The antioxidant and anti-inflammatory benefits of flaxseeds cover nearly every system of the body. They've been shown to help regulate our cardiovascular health, prevent cancer, maintain our digestive health, balance our blood sugar, keep our vascular system healthy, and even help balance hormone levels in postmenopausal women.

AVAILABILITY

Ground flaxseed meal is available at many supermarkets, but because of the high levels of fatty acids, the ground meal may break down and go rancid on store shelves. For the freshest and tastiest flax, buy whole flaxseeds and grind them yourself in a coffee grinder, or buy ground flaxseed meal from a chiller case and store it in an opaque container in the fridge or freezer.

HOW TO USE

In its whole seed form, flax is difficult for many people to digest, and therefore its health benefits aren't nearly as strong versus those in ground flaxseed meal. To get the most of out your flax, grind it before consuming.

Ground or whole flax-seeds can be used as a topping for yogurt or cereal, in place of flours or seeds in baked goods, and as a superfood addition to smoothies.

NUTRITION HIGHLIGHTS PER 1 TABLESPOON GROUND FLAXSEEDS

QUINOA

If there is one superfood that has skyrocketed in popularity overnight, it's quinoa! A decade ago, you would have struggled to find quinoa at even the biggest health food store, but now you can find quinoa on the shelves at almost every grocery store, plus in cereals, baked goods, and desserts.

QUICK FACTS

❶ Quinoa is considered one of the world's most perfect foods for its balance between fat, protein, and whole-grain fiber, as well as its richness of nutrients.

❷ Quinoa is a good complete source of vegetarian protein.

HEALTH BENEFITS

Quinoa (pronounced "keen-wah") is a great plant-based source of complete protein—meaning it contains all the essential amino acids the body needs.

In general, quinoa is considered one of the most nutrient-dense foods on the planet. Thought to be one of nature's "most-perfect foods," quinoa not only provides healthy whole-grain fiber, like most whole-grain cereals, but also a decent amount of healthy fats, complete protein, and a wide variety of vitamins and minerals.

AVAILABILITY

Look for quinoa in the rice or whole-grains section of your local grocery store. You can also find quinoa in the bulk bins at many health food stores.

HOW TO USE

Cook quinoa just as you would rice, using a two-to-one liquid-to-grain ratio. Quinoa is packed with lots of intricate flavors, so you might not need to add any salt or flavorings.

QUINOA BREAKFAST PORRIDGE

Who says oatmeal is the only grain you can have for breakfast? Quinoa is frequently reserved for a dinner side dish, but this breakfast-friendly recipe is creamy, lightly sweet, and packed full of fiber and vegetarian protein.

MAKES: *2 large servings*
TIME: *30 minutes*

1 cup quinoa, rinsed

2 cups milk

Pinch of salt

2 tablespoons honey

2 tablespoons pure maple syrup

¼ teaspoon ground cinnamon

½ teaspoon vanilla extract

Your favorite toppings
(raisins, chopped nuts, brown sugar, etc.)

In a medium-size saucepan, combine the quinoa, milk, salt, honey, maple syrup, and cinnamon. Bring to a boil over medium-high heat, lower the heat, and simmer until the quinoa has absorbed most of the liquid, about 20 minutes. Remove from the heat and stir in the vanilla. Divide between two bowls and top with your favorite toppings.

NUTRITION PER SERVING (NOT INCLUDING TOPPINGS): 504 CALORIES, 4.9 G FAT, 94.4 G CARBS, 19.4 G PROTEIN

THIS PORRIDGE IS DELICIOUS HOT OR COLD.
TRY MAKING A BIG BATCH OF IT ON THE
WEEKEND AND DOLING IT OUT COLD FOR A
QUICK BREAKFAST THROUGHOUT THE WEEK.

SPINACH-AVOCADO SMOOTHIE

Your first reaction to the ingredients in this smoothie might be "yuck!" but I promise this smoothie is worth your time. Once blended up with banana and peanut butter, both the avocado and spinach are totally undetectable flavor-wise. And the avocado gives the smoothie an incredible creamy, silky texture. This smoothie is a great meal-replacement drink because it's got an excellent balance of lean protein, healthy fats, and all-natural carbs.

MAKES: *2 servings*
TIME: *5 minutes*

1 avocado, pitted and scooped from skin

1 cup fresh spinach

1 large, ripe banana

1 tablespoon natural peanut butter

1 cup milk

Handful of ice cubes

Blend all the ingredients in a blender on high speed until very smooth. Pour into two glasses and serve immediately.

NUTRITION PER SERVING: 380 CALORIES, 26.2 G FAT, 32.2 G CARBS, 9.5 G PROTEIN

TRY ADDING HALF OF AN AVOCADO TO ANY OF YOUR FAVORITE SMOOTHIE CONCOCTIONS; THE ADDED FAT HELPS KEEP YOU FEELING FULL AND THE SMOOTH AND CREAMY TEXTURE IS TOP-NOTCH!

BANANA WALNUT WHOLE WHEAT PANCAKES

Just because you're eating a superfood diet doesn't mean you have to skip the big ole stack of fluffy pancakes for breakfast! These pancakes are 100 percent whole grain and packed full of nutty, banana flavor.

MAKES: 4 servings
TIME: 30 minutes

1 cup buttermilk

1 tablespoon honey

1 large egg

1 teaspoon vanilla extract

2 tablespoons melted butter

1 cup white whole wheat flour

½ teaspoon baking powder

¼ teaspoon baking soda

Pinch salt

1 teaspoon ground cinnamon

2 ripe bananas, sliced thinly

½ cup chopped walnuts

Preheat a nonstick griddle or skillet over medium-high heat. In a small mixing bowl, whisk together the buttermilk, honey, egg, vanilla, and melted butter until smooth. In a large mixing bowl, sift together the flour, baking powder, baking soda, salt, and cinnamon. Pour the wet ingredients into the dry, and stir until just mixed—there should still be some lumps. Pour ⅓ cup of the batter onto the heated griddle, place a few banana slices on the pancake batter, and sprinkle with a bit of the chopped walnuts. Let cook until the edges look set and bubbles begin to form, about 3 minutes. Flip and continue to cook for an additional minute. Continue with the remaining batter, banana slices, and walnuts.

NUTRITION PER SERVING: 361 CALORIES, 17.1 G FAT, 44.2 G CARBS, 11.8 G PROTEIN

YOU MIGHT BE TEMPTED TO SUB IN REGULAR MILK FOR THE BUTTERMILK HERE, BUT I RECOMMEND YOU STICK WITH THE BUTTERMILK. THE ACIDITY OF THE BUTTERMILK HELPS CUT THE WHOLE-GRAIN FLAVOR OF THE WHOLE WHEAT FLOUR, MAKING IT TASTE MORE LIKE A "REGULAR" PANCAKE.

BANANA CREAM PIE SMOOTHIE

This smoothie is deceiving—it tastes like a decadent dessert, but is packed with tons of healthy nutrients to keep your fueled for the day. Serve this up for breakfast or as a late afternoon pick-me-up.

MAKES: *2 servings*
TIME: *5 minutes*

1 ripe banana, frozen

1 cup plain, low-fat Greek yogurt

½ teaspoon vanilla extract

2 tablespoons honey

⅓ cup unsweetened nut, soy, or cow's milk

Handful of ice cubes

Graham cracker crumbs, crushed, for garnish

Combine the banana, yogurt, vanilla, honey, milk, and ice in a blender. Blend on high speed until smooth. Pour into two glasses and sprinkle graham cracker crumbs on top before serving.

NUTRITION PER SERVING: 443 CALORIES, 13.6 G FAT, 49.1 G CARBS, 31.4 G PROTEIN

2

LUNCH

CILANTRO-AVOCADO AMARANTH SALAD

If you're new to this earthy whole grain, the rich flavor of amaranth might take some getting used to—and this salad is a great place to start! The flavorful mix-ins and dressing work in harmony with the strong, peppery flavor of the amaranth. This is an amazing side dish for Mexican foods (I like serving it with the tacos on page 132).

MAKES: *8 servings*
TIME: *30 minutes (plus chilling time)*

2 cups chicken or vegetable broth

1 cup amaranth

1 red bell pepper, seeded and diced

½ large red onion, diced

1 cup cherry tomatoes, halved

1 cup fresh cilantro, minced

2 tablespoons extra-virgin olive oil

1 tablespoon red wine vinegar

Zest and juice of 1 lime

1 teaspoon minced fresh garlic

1 teaspoon honey

½ teaspoon salt

½ teaspoon ground black pepper

1 teaspoon ground cumin

1 avocado, peeled, pitted, and diced

Bring the broth to a boil over medium-high heat in a medium-size saucepan. Once at a boil, whisk in the amaranth, bring back to a boil, lower the heat, and simmer until the amaranth is tender and the liquid has been absorbed, about 25 minutes. Fluff the amaranth with a fork, and then transfer to a medium-size mixing bowl. Add the bell pepper, onion, tomatoes, and cilantro to the amaranth, and toss to combine. In a small bowl, whisk together the olive oil, vinegar, lime zest and juice, garlic, honey, salt, ground pepper, and cumin until combined. Pour over the amaranth mixture and stir to combine. Refrigerate the mixture until cold, about an hour. Stir in the diced avocado just before serving.

NUTRITION PER SERVING: 199 CALORIES, 10.5 G FAT, 22.2 G CARBS, 5.7 G PROTEIN

THE TEXTURE OF THE AMARANTH ALSO MAKES THIS
A FUN (AND TASTY) DIP FOR TORTILLA CHIPS!

AMARANTH

An ancient whole grain that is packed with flavor and nutrition, amaranth is a food that was reintroduced to North America in the 1970s after a lengthy exile from healthy diets. This gluten-free grain can be used in recipes in place of rice, quinoa, or any other whole grain.

QUICK FACTS

1 An ancient whole grain, amaranth has many health benefits similar to those of dark, leafy greens.

2 Amaranth has a nutty, earthy flavor that can be intensified by popping the grain like popcorn.

3 Amaranth is rich in amino acids that are missing from many other whole grains.

HEALTH BENEFITS

While amaranth is considered a grain, its nutritional profile (and flavor) is more like that of dark, leafy greens, such as chard and kale. Amaranth is rich in amino acids that aren't found in many other grains. It also contains more calcium, iron, and magnesium than do similar whole grains.

AVAILABILITY

Since amaranth was only introduced to North American households relatively recently, it can be hard to track down. Try checking the bulk bins at your local health food store.

HOW TO USE

Like other whole grains, amaranth can be simmered with water or broth until it's fluffy and tender. You can also pop amaranth in a skillet, similar to popcorn!

NUTRITION HIGHLIGHTS PER 1 CUP COOKED AMARANTH

251	4g	46g	9g	29%	21%	12%
CALORIES	FAT	CARBS	PROTEIN	IRON	DIETARY FIBER	CALCIUM

CABBAGE

It might seem strange to have the lowly cabbage on a list of the world's most nutritious foods, but cabbage doesn't get the respect it deserves! Try adding more cabbage to your diet to see some incredible health benefits.

QUICK FACTS

1 Cabbage is one of the best available foods for its anticancer benefits.

2 Both red and green cabbage have different and important nutritional benefits.

3 Lightly steaming cabbage seems to bring out its cholesterol-lowering compounds.

HEALTH BENEFITS

The deep red and purple color of red cabbage is an indicator that it is packed with polyphenols (which are also in green cabbage, just not in as high a concentration). These polyphenols help make cabbage one of the best anticancer foods on store shelves. In fact, studies have shown that both red and green cabbage have different cancer-fighting compounds, so get your fill of both!

AVAILABILITY

Red and green cabbage are both found year-round in grocery stores, and are usually available during the cooler weather months at your local farmers' market. Select cabbage heads whose leaves are tightly bound—that indicates the freshest heads.

HOW TO USE

Cabbage is one of the few superfoods whose nutrition profile increases with cooking. Studies show that steaming or sautéing, in particular, may help bring out the cholesterol-lowering ability of cabbage. However, eating raw cabbage is the best way to get the most out of cabbage's anticancer benefits.

NUTRITION HIGHLIGHTS PER 1 CUP SHREDDED, RAW CABBAGE

17	0.1g	4.1g	1g	42%	7%	5%
CALORIES	FAT	CARBS	PROTEIN	VITAMIN C	DIETARY FIBER	VITAMIN B6

BARLEY CABBAGE ROLLS

Usually, cabbage rolls are stuffed with a flavorful meat filling before baking, but these rolls use the chewy, nutty flavor and texture of barley to make them a hearty, satisfying dish without the meat.

THIS ISN'T A QUICK DINNER, BUT THE
SLOW-COOKED TASTE IS WORTH THE EFFORT!

MAKES: 8 servings
TIME: 1 hour 15 minutes

2 cups barley

4 cups vegetable broth

1 head cabbage

1 tablespoon butter

2 cloves garlic, minced

1 large onion, diced

1 large green bell pepper,
seeded and diced

1 teaspoon Italian seasoning

½ cup ketchup

½ teaspoon fennel seeds

2 tablespoons maple syrup or brown sugar

2 tablespoons cider vinegar

2 tablespoons Worcestershire sauce

8 ounces cream cheese, softened

Salt and pepper

2 (14-ounce) cans diced tomatoes

Preheat the oven to 350°F. Combine the barley and broth in a medium-size saucepan over high heat. Bring to a boil, lower the heat, and simmer until the barley is tender and the liquid has been absorbed, about 20 minutes. Set aside.

Fill a large stockpot with water and bring to a boil, then drop in the entire head of cabbage and cook until the outer leaves are tender and bright green, about 10 minutes. Remove the cabbage from the water and drain on paper towels. Once cool enough to handle, pull off the large outer leaves and cut out the base of the thick stem. Dice the remaining cabbage and set aside.

Meanwhile, heat the butter in a large skillet or Dutch oven over medium heat. Once melted, add the garlic and cook until fragrant and tender, about 3 minutes. Then add the onion and green peppers and cook until tender, about 10 minutes. Add the remaining diced cabbage, Italian seasoning, ketchup, fennel seeds, maple syrup, vinegar, Worcestershire sauce, cream cheese, and salt and pepper to taste. Lower the heat to low and simmer for 10 minutes before adding to the barley. In a blender, puree the diced tomatoes until very smooth.

To assemble the cabbage rolls, pour a small amount of the tomato puree on the bottom of a 9 x 13-inch casserole dish. For each roll, put about ½ cup of the barley mixture in the middle of one of the cabbage leaves. Roll up tightly and place in the prepared casserole dish. Continue with the remaining leaves, until the casserole dish is full. Pour the remaining tomato sauce over the top of the rolls. Bake for 40 to 45 minutes, or until bubbly and browned. Remove from the oven and let rest for 10 to 15 minutes before serving.

NUTRITION PER SERVING: 362 CALORIES,
14 G FAT, 51 G CARBS, 11 G PROTEIN

SPINACH & FETA SALAD
with Blueberry-Balsamic Vinaigrette

This salad gets you a double punch of healthy blueberry goodness. So often, side salads are the sad, boring, compulsory part of a meal—but this salad is good enough to stand on its own. Creamy feta and crunchy roasted pecans help balance the earthy flavor of the spinach greens and the tang of the blueberries.

MAKES: 4 servings
TIME: 10 minutes

For the dressing

¾ cup fresh blueberries

Juice of 1 lime

¼ cup balsamic vinegar

⅓ cup extra-virgin olive oil

2 tablespoons honey

2 teaspoons Dijon mustard

½ teaspoon salt

For the salad

½ cup pecan halves

8 cups baby spinach

4 ounces crumbled feta cheese

½ cup diced red onion

1 cup fresh blueberries

To prepare the dressing, combine all the dressing ingredients in a blender. Blend on high speed until emulsified, about 30 seconds. Set aside.

To prepare the salad, in a medium-size nonstick skillet over medium-high heat, toast the pecan halves until fragrant and slightly browned, about 5 minutes. Remove from the heat. Combine the spinach, feta, pecans, red onion, and blueberries in a large bowl (or divide among four plates for single servings). Drizzle with the vinaigrette.

NUTRITION PER SERVING: 370 CALORIES, 29.7 G FAT, 22.6 G CARBS, 8.0 G PROTEIN

TOP THIS SALAD WITH SOME GRILLED CHICKEN BREAST FOR A DELICIOUS AND HEALTHY LUNCH OPTION.

IF YOU HAVE A HARD
TIME TRACKING
DOWN CASHEW
BUTTER, YOU CAN
SUB IN TAHINI OR
UNSWEETENED
NATURAL PEANUT
BUTTER IN THE
DRESSING.

CABBAGE CASHEW CHICKEN SALAD

This is such a fun twist on your typical chicken salad! It's packed with veggies, making it a great option for a one-bowl lunch.

MAKES: 8 servings
TIME: 30 minutes

For the dressing

1 tablespoon sesame oil

1 tablespoon olive oil

1 tablespoon rice vinegar

3 tablespoons cashew butter

Juice and zest of 1 lime

2 tablespoons finely minced fresh cilantro

2 teaspoons honey

Salt and pepper

For the salad

½ head green cabbage, shredded or sliced thinly

2 cups chopped cooked chicken

2 green onions, sliced

1 cup shredded carrot

½ cup seeded and julienned red bell pepper (about ½ large pepper)

1 cup mandarin orange segments (canned or fresh)

½ cup roughly chopped cashews

To prepare the dressing, in a small bowl, whisk together all the dressing ingredients until smooth.

To prepare the salad, in a large mixing bowl, combine all the salad ingredients and toss until well mixed. Pour the dressing over the top, and toss to coat. Serve immediately, or let the flavors meld for 30 minutes in fridge for the best flavor.

NUTRITION PER SERVING: 216 CALORIES, 12.3 G FAT, 13.4 G CARBS, 14.0 G PROTEIN

BLT+AE SANDWICH

It's hard to imagine improving on the classic BLT sandwich, but I think this pumped-up version gives it a run for its money. By adding creamy, smooth avocado and panfried eggs to these, you get a sandwich that feels like a hearty meal, worthy of way more than just lunch.

MAKES: 4 sandwiches
TIME: 15 minutes

4 large eggs

1 whole wheat baguette

8 slices bacon, cooked

2 tomatoes, sliced thinly

1 head romaine lettuce

1 avocado, pitted, peeled, and sliced thinly

Salt and pepper

Heat a nonstick skillet over medium-high heat. Crack in the eggs, break the yolks, and cook for about 2 minutes, then flip over and cook for an additional minute, until the eggs are cooked through. Slice the baguette into four equal pieces, and then slice the pieces in half lengthwise. To assemble the sandwiches, place two slices of bacon, one-quarter of the tomato slices, one-quarter of the lettuce, and one-quarter of the avocado slices on the bottom half of each of the baguette pieces. Top with the egg and season with salt and pepper to taste. Top with the remaining half of the baguette.

NUTRITION PER SERVING: 671 CALORIES, 32.0 G FAT, 64.2 G CARBS, 33.1 G PROTEIN

FOR A SMALLER SANDWICH THAT'S PERFECT FOR SERVING TO A GROUP, CUT THE BAGUETTE INTO EIGHT SLICES BEFORE ASSEMBLY.

EGGS

A few years back, eggs took a reputation hit for being high in cholesterol, but now we know that they are one of the healthiest (and most affordable) sources of lean protein on the market. Eggs aren't just for breakfast anymore!

QUICK FACTS

1. A powerful source of omega-3s, eggs may help regulate cholesterol and reduce the risk of many disorders and diseases of the mind.
2. The type of egg you buy matters—look for pasture-raised eggs for the most nutritional bang for your buck.
3. Eggs are a good source of two minerals that are lacking from many North American diets—selenium and iodine.

HEALTH BENEFITS

To get the most health benefits from an egg, you need to eat the whole thing. Egg yolks contain a very high concentration of omega-3 fatty acids, which are vital to help maintain healthy levels of triglycerides, blood cholesterol, and blood pressure. They also may help protect us from disorders and diseases of the brain, such as ADHD, Alzheimer's, dementia, and depression. The type of egg you buy matters. While all eggs contain omega-3s, free-range or pasture-raised chickens lay eggs with the highest concentration of omega-3s.

Beyond their impressive omega-3 concentration, eggs are also an excellent source of powerful lean protein. Eggs contain all the B vitamins and are a good source of both selenium and iodine, two minerals that many people struggle to get enough of.

AVAILABILITY

Eggs are a staple in many North American kitchens, but not all eggs are created equal. Look for organic, free-range or pasture-raised eggs for the highest nutritional profile. (Bonus: They usually taste better and can be more affordable when purchased from local farmers.)

HOW TO USE

Hard-boiled, scrambled, over easy—everyone has a favorite way of eating eggs! Making eggs a staple of your diet is simple once you figure out what method of cooking appeals to you best.

MUSHROOMS

The varieties of sizes, flavors, and textures of mushrooms means that there is inevitably a mushroom out there for every person's tastes. And the health benefits of a diet rich in mushrooms mean you should definitely start using them as more than just a pizza topping.

QUICK FACTS

1 Mushrooms helps protect and strengthen our white blood cells, which helps make for a strong immune system.

2 Mushrooms are packed with anti-inflammatory compounds that help reduce the risk of many inflammation-related illnesses.

3 In particular, mushrooms have been shown to help prevent certain hormone-related cancers, such as cancer of the breast and prostate.

HEALTH BENEFITS

Studies have shown that a wide variety of mushrooms (including regular button mushrooms) support our immune systems, thanks to the compounds in mushrooms that help balance the health of our white blood cells, the building blocks to our immune system.

Mushrooms are also packed with anti-inflammatory compounds, meaning they can help reduce the risk of many inflammation-related diseases, including type 2 diabetes, cardiovascular disease, and cancer. In particular, it seems that certain compounds in mushrooms might help target hormone-related cancers, such as cancers of the breast and prostate.

AVAILABILITY

You can find button mushrooms at nearly every grocery store, but you might have to look a little harder to track down a wider variety of mushrooms. If you aren't a fan of the white button kind, try looking for such interesting and different varieties as Portobello, cremini, morel, shiitake, chanterelle, and oyster mushrooms.

HOW TO USE

Store mushrooms in the fridge to keep their powerful health compounds intact for the longest period of time. Because mushrooms have a spongelike quality, the best way to clean them is to wipe off debris with a damp cloth instead of running them under water. Sautéing mushrooms brings out the best flavor, and helps reduce some of the moisture in the mushrooms.

NUTRITION HIGHLIGHTS PER 1 CUP MUSHROOMS

21	0.3g	3.7g	0.8g	40%	34%	27%
CALORIES	FAT	CARBS	PROTEIN	COPPER	SELENIUM	VITAMIN B2

MUSHROOM, CORN & BLACK BEAN FARRO

While farro is a wheat product and does contain gluten, the structure of the grain makes this gluten easier to digest for many folks with gluten sensitivities (still avoid if you have celiac disease or an allergy). Because it's so easy to digest (and so tasty), this farro salad is a great option for pot lucks!

MAKES: 6 servings
TIME: 25 minutes

1 cup farro

2 cups vegetable broth

1 tablespoon olive oil

1 medium-size onion, diced

3 cloves garlic, minced

8 ounces baby bella mushrooms, sliced

1 teaspoon ground cumin

2 cups frozen corn

Salt and pepper

1 14-ounce can black beans, drained and rinsed

½ cup finely chopped fresh cilantro

Juice of ½ lime

In a medium-size saucepan, combine the farro and broth. Bring to a boil over high heat, lower the heat to low, and simmer until all the broth is absorbed. Meanwhile, heat the olive oil in a skillet over medium-low heat. Add the onion and garlic and cook until tender, about 3 minutes. Add the mushrooms, cumin, corn, and salt and pepper to taste and cook until the mushrooms are soft, about 7 minutes. Remove from the heat. In a large bowl, combine the cooked farro, mushroom mixture, black beans, cilantro, and lime juice, then toss. Serve warm or chill for an hour and serve cold.

NUTRITION PER SERVING: 319 CALORIES, 4.4 G FAT, 58 G CARBS, 15.9 G PROTEIN

YOU CAN SUB IN OTHER WHOLE-GRAIN SUPERFOODS IN THIS DISH IF YOU'RE HAVING TROUBLE TRACKING DOWN FARRO— TRY QUINOA, BARLEY, OR FREEKEH!

THE GINGER FLAVOR IN THIS SOUP IS A SUBTLE WARMTH IN THE
BACKGROUND; ADD MORE GINGER IF YOU'D LIKE MORE OF A BITE!

GINGERED COCONUT & CARROT BISQUE

If you hear that a dish is vegan and gluten-free, your first reaction might be that it's probably taste-free, too. But that's not the case with this spicy, sweet, creamy soup! It has so much powerful flavor that you won't miss the cream.

MAKES: 4 servings
TIME: 30 minutes

1 tablespoon olive oil

1 large onion, diced

2 cloves garlic, minced

2 tablespoons minced fresh ginger

2 pounds carrots, chopped roughly

4 cups vegetable broth

1 (13-ounce) can light coconut milk

1 to 2 chili peppers, seeded and chopped

1 teaspoon lime juice

Salt and pepper

Heat the olive oil in a soup pot over medium-high heat. Add the onion, garlic, and ginger and cook until just soft and translucent, about 5 minutes. Add the carrots, broth, coconut milk, and chili peppers. Bring to a boil, lower the heat, and simmer for 20 to 25 minutes, or until the carrots are fork tender. Remove from the heat. Puree the soup in batches in a blender or use an immersion blender until perfectly smooth.

Just before serving, stir in the lime juice, and salt and pepper to taste.

NUTRITION PER SERVING: 256 CALORIES, 11.6 G FAT, 33.2 G CARBS, 9.1 G PROTEIN

BOK CHOY & APPLE SLAW WITH GOJI BERRIES

It seems as if every family has a go-to slaw recipe for picnics, pot lucks, and barbecues. We do, too, but ours is a little bit out of the ordinary! Instead of the standard cabbage, I love using crunchy, green bok choy and tart apples as a base. When combined with sweet, chewy goji berries and a sweet and tangy dressing, you've got a slaw that'll turn heads.

MAKES: 4 servings
TIME: 15 minutes (plus chilling time)

½ cup dried goji berries

1 cup hot water

1 pound bok choy (about 1 large head), julienned

3 green onions, sliced thinly

1 tart apple, Granny Smith preferred, cored and julienned

2 large stalks celery, julienned

1 large carrot, peeled and shredded

1 teaspoon poppy seeds

⅓ cup low-fat, plain Greek yogurt

¼ cup mayonnaise

2 tablespoons cider vinegar

2 tablespoons honey

½ teaspoon salt

½ teaspoon ground black pepper

In a small bowl, combine the goji berries and hot water. In a large bowl, mix together the bok choy, green onions, apple, celery, carrot, and poppy seeds until well combined. Drain the softened goji berries, squeezing out and discarding any excess water, and add to the bok choy mixture. In a small bowl, whisk together the yogurt, mayonnaise, vinegar, honey, salt, and pepper. Pour the dressing over the bok choy mixture, and toss to coat. Chill for at least 30 minutes before serving.

NUTRITION PER SERVING: 210 CALORIES, 7.0 G FAT, 35.2 G CARBS, 4.7 G PROTEIN

THIS SLAW USES THE ENTIRE HEAD OF BOK CHOY—CRUNCHY STEM AND SOFT LEAVES— TO ADD A FUN MIX OF TEXTURES AND COLORS.

APPLE

Apples might just be the quintessential health food. After all, the whole "An apple a day..." saying isn't just a catchphrase—apples really are packed with tons of nutrients that can help keep you healthy— and maybe just keep the doctor away.

QUICK FACTS

❶ Packed full of antioxidants that help regulate blood sugar, prevent cancer, fight cardiovascular disease, and reduce the risk of asthma.

❷ For the most nutritional benefits, keep the skin on.

HEALTH BENEFITS

Recent research has indicated that apples are a particularly strong method for regulating blood sugar and helping to prevent diabetes. Flavonoids in apples help slow down the digestions of carbohydrates; polyphenols reduce glucose absorption, plus help signal the pancreas to release more insulin, and keep blood sugars balanced. Just as in most other fruits, the antioxidants in apples are also powerful cancer-fighting compounds. These same antioxidants have also been shown in studies to help lower the risk of asthma and cardiovascular disease.

AVAILABILITY

You can pick up a wide variety of both organic and conventionally grown apples at most supermarkets all year long. For the highest concentration of antioxidants, look for apples with dark red or pink skin. Don't worry; if yellow or green apples are your favorite, they still have lots of health benefits, just not in the same high concentration as the deep-colored ones.

HOW TO USE

To get the most nutritional bang for your buck, don't peel your apples. The highest concentration of antioxidants is found in the skins. It's best to eat apples in their whole form—although applesauce and apple juice do provide some nutrients, their nutrient profile is greatly diminished from that of the whole fruit.

GRAPEFRUIT

It's not breaking news that grapefruit is a health food. Diets that are heavy in grapefruit have been making the rounds for decades. But the true extent of the health benefits of these super citrus fruits is just starting to be revealed.

QUICK FACTS

1 Eat more grapefruit to help prevent and shorten colds; they're packed with immune-boosting vitamin C.

2 Pink and red grapefruit contain the cancer-fighting antioxidant lycopene, particularly effective in its ability to prevent prostate cancer.

3 Eat grapefruit raw or drink fresh grapefruit juice to get the most health benefits.

HEALTH BENEFITS

If you want to make sure you log enough of the immune-boosting vitamin C, grapefruit are for you. Over 20 scientific studies have shown that a boost of vitamin C can help reduce the length and severity of the cold virus. Vitamin C also is a power anti-inflammatory, helping relieve the symptoms of asthma and arthritis.

Pink and red grapefruit are packed with the antioxidant lycopene, which has been shown to have tumor-fighting compounds. In fact, a diet rich in lycopene-heavy foods has been shown to lower a man's risk of prostate cancer.

AVAILABILITY

Both organic and conventionally grown grapefruit are available year-round in most supermarkets, but for the best sweetness and flavor, look for them when they're in season during the winter. Winter grapefruit are a great way to add an in-season burst of fresh fruit during an otherwise lacking fruit season.

HOW TO USE

Fully ripened grapefruit have the highest level of antioxidants (and, not so coincidentally, the highest level of flavor), so keep an eye out for firm, ripe fruit. Eat grapefruit fresh by cutting the flesh away from the bitter pith, and scooping it out with a spoon or grapefruit tool.

While many experts agree on avoiding sugar-heavy fruit juices, studies have shown that grapefruit juice is the exception to the rule. The tangy juice is packed with a high dose of antioxidants and nourishing vitamins and minerals.

NUTRITION HIGHLIGHTS PER ½ GRAPEFRUIT

52	0.2g	13g	1g	64%	29%	5%
CALORIES	FAT	CARBS	PROTEIN	VITAMIN C	VITAMIN A	VITAMIN B6

CITRUS MINT SALAD

There is something incredibly beautiful in the simplicity of this salad. It's just some citrus fruit tossed with a simple, sweet dressing and a minced, fresh herb. But the flavors blend together incredibly well, and the colors and textures are hard to beat.

MAKES: 4 servings
TIME: 10 minutes

2 grapefruit, segmented

4 tangerines, segmented

3 oranges, segmented

Juice and zest of 1 lemon

1 tablespoon honey

1 ½ teaspoons chopped fresh mint

In a medium-size bowl, toss together the grapefruit, tangerine, and orange segments. In a small bowl, whisk together the lemon juice, lemon zest, honey, and mint. Pour the dressing over the citrus segments and toss to coat.

NUTRITION PER SERVING: 151 CALORIES, 0.3 G FAT, 38.9 G CARBS, 2.8 G PROTEIN

THIS IS A GREAT SALAD TO SERVE FOR BRUNCH!

SUNSHINE SALAD
with Green Tea Vinaigrette

This salad lives up to its name: it's bright, sunny, and full of light flavor! Matcha powder is a great way to add green tea flavor (and nutrition) to your cooking—look for it in the tea section of your local health food store.

MAKES: 2 servings
TIME: 5 minutes

For the vinaigrette

¼ cup extra-virgin olive oil

1 teaspoon matcha green tea powder

Juice of 1 lemon

Salt and pepper

For the salad

1 cup baby spinach

1 cup chopped romaine lettuce

½ cup mandarin orange segments

½ cup sprouts (lentil is great)

¼ cup sliced red onion

2 tablespoons pine nuts

To prepare the vinaigrette, whisk together all the vinaigrette ingredients until smooth.

To prepare the salad, in a large bowl, combine the salad ingredients. Drizzle with the vinaigrette.

NUTRITION PER SERVING: 352 CALORIES, 31.5 G FAT, 19.2 G CARBS, 4.3 G PROTEIN

GREEN POWER SALAD

I like to eat a wide variety of colors in my diet, because it's a great way to make sure I'm getting a wide variety of healthy nutrients, but this monochromic salad keeps it green and still packs a nutritious punch.

MAKES: 1 serving
TIME: 10 minutes

1 cup spinach

1 cup chopped romaine lettuce

½ cup baby kale

½ cucumber, sliced

¼ avocado, peeled and sliced

1 green onion, sliced

1 tablespoon hemp seeds

Juice of ½ lemon

1 tablespoon extra-virgin olive oil

Salt and pepper

Combine the spinach, romaine, kale, cucumber, avocado, green onion, and hemp seeds in a large bowl. Squeeze on the lemon juice and drizzle with the olive oil. Season with salt and pepper to taste.

NUTRITION PER SERVING: 331 CALORIES, 28.3 G FAT, 17.6 G CARBS, 7.3 G PROTEIN

KEEP WITH THE GREEN THEME AND TRY THESE OTHER SUPERFOOD ADD-INS: PUMPKIN SEEDS, LENTIL SPROUTS, OR SLICED GREEN GRAPES.

GREEN TEA

Turn on the TV lately, and it seems as if there is always a new study touting the benefits of regular consumption of green tea. Tea is the most popular beverage in the world and was reportedly discovered as early as 2737 BC.

QUICK FACTS

❶ Green tea is loaded with the powerful antioxidant epigallocatechin gallate (EGCG).

❷ Green tea has been shown to help regulate blood pressure, help people maintain a healthy weight, and fight many cancers.

HEALTH BENEFITS

Because green tea is the least processed version of the beverage made from the tea plant, it contains the most antioxidants of all the teas. One of the most researched is epigallocatechin gallate (EGCG), which has been attributed as the source of many of green tea's health benefits.

Research has shown that EGCG is a powerful anticancer compound that limits the growth of tumors of the stomach, lungs, liver, breast, and colon. EGCG has also been shown to help promote healthy weight loss, control type 2 diabetes, and balance blood pressure.

AVAILABILITY

Green tea is available in loose leaf and bag form at most supermarkets and coffee shops. While bagged green tea is beneficial, to get the highest concentration of antioxidants, brewing loose leaf tea is the way to go.

HOW TO USE

Brew green tea just as you would any other tea (following the timing and water temperature directions for your particular type of green), but matcha—powdered green tea—can also be a great way to add the green tea flavor and health benefits to other dishes.

NUTRITION HIGHLIGHTS PER 1 CUP BREWED GREEN TEA

0	0g	0g	0g
CALORIES	FAT	CARBS	PROTEIN

KALE

Ah, kale. The darling of healthy foods! It's become so popular over the past few years that there are even T-shirts and bumper stickers imploring people to eat more of it! Kale deserves all of its popularity. This dark, leafy green is easy to find, delicious, and packed with health benefits.

QUICK FACTS

❶ Kale has a unique combination of antioxidants that have been proven to stop cells from turning cancerous.

❷ This green is an important addition to the diet of those who are looking to lower their cholesterol.

❸ Kale is available during the cold-weather months, when many other fruits and vegetables are not in season.

HEALTH BENEFITS

Like many of its dark, leafy, green friends in the produce aisle, kale has been researched extensively for its anticancer compounds. In particular, kale contains a unique combination of carotenoids and flavonoids that have been shown to help prevent the cells in our body from becoming cancerous.

Kale is also a powerful ally in our fight against high blood cholesterol. The cholesterol-lowering benefits of kale are present whether it is raw or cooked.

AVAILABILITY

With kale's jump in popularity over the past decade, it's common to find both organic and conventionally grown kale on the produce shelves at your local supermarket. You may even be able to pick up multiple varieties of kale to help you decide which version of this green works best for you.

Like many other dark, leafy greens, kale thrives in cold and cooler weather—in fact, this green is so hardy it will grow right through a snowstorm! Use this fact to your advantage and stock up on kale during the cold-weather months when other fruits and veggies aren't as abundant.

HOW TO USE

Many folks find the texture and taste of kale to be a bit off-putting when eaten raw, but if you "massage" the leaves, the fibers loosen and become easier to chew, and the flavor becomes less intense. Kale also holds up beautifully to cooking: The texture softens and the flavor becomes milder, but it still retains some of its "chew." Try popping kale in a preheated 350°F oven for 15 to 20 minutes to get crunchy, crispy kale chips that might satisfy a chip craving.

LEMON-AVOCADO RAW KALE SALAD

This massaged-kale salad is incredibly simple, but the process of massaging the dressing into the kale makes the flavor and texture taste way more complex than the ingredient list indicates.

MAKES: *2 servings*
TIME: *5 minutes*

1 bunch kale, stems removed and torn into bite-size pieces

½ ripe avocado, pitted

Juice of ½ lemon

Salt and pepper

Toasted sesame seeds for garnish

Place the kale in a large bowl. Using clean hands, squeeze the avocado flesh into the bowl and massage the avocado into the kale until the leaves relax and are all coated in avocado—about 5 minutes. Squeeze in the lemon juice, season with salt and pepper to taste, and then toss to coat. Sprinkle with sesame seeds, if using.

NUTRITION PER SERVING: 169 CALORIES, 9.8 G FAT, 18.4 G CARBS, 5.0 G PROTEIN

MAKE SURE TO REALLY GET IN THERE WITH YOUR FINGERS AND MASSAGE THOSE KALE LEAVES. THIS ISN'T A JOB FOR A SPOON!

CHEF SALAD
with Kefir Ranch Dressing

The texture and tang of kefir makes it a perfect base for this healthy ranch dressing. I like to pour it on top of a classic chef's salad, but it also makes an awesome veggie dip or pizza sauce.

MAKES: *1 large dinner salad*
TIME: *15 minutes (plus chilling time)*

For the dressing

1 ½ cups plain kefir

½ teaspoon dried chives

½ teaspoon dried parsley

1 teaspoon dried dill

1 teaspoon garlic powder

1 teaspoon onion powder

½ teaspoon salt

¼ teaspoon ground black pepper

For the salad

1 head romaine lettuce, chopped

1 ounce Cheddar cheese, diced

1 ounce smoked turkey breast, sliced

1 ounce ham, sliced

1 large hard-boiled egg, chopped

1 green onion, sliced thinly

½ cup cherry tomatoes, halved

¼ avocado, peeled and diced

¼ cucumber, chopped

To prepare the dressing, whisk together all the dressing ingredients until smooth. Refrigerate for at least an hour to allow the flavors to meld.

To assemble the salad, place all the salad ingredients in a large bowl and drizzle with the ranch dressing.

NUTRITION PER SERVING: 525 CALORIES, 31.1 G FAT, 38.2 G CARBS, 34.7 G PROTEIN

THIS DRESSING RECIPE MAKES ENOUGH FOR FOUR TO SIX SALAD SERVINGS, SO STASH IT IN THE FRIDGE FOR THE NEXT TIME YOU NEED RANCH DRESSING.

KEFIR

The health benefits of eating a diet rich in probiotics has been well documented, but one probiotic-rich beverage hasn't quite made it into the spotlight—kefir. Kefir is a fermented dairy product that is tangy like yogurt, slightly carbonated, and packed with tummy-friendly probiotics.

QUICK FACTS

1. Packed with healthy bacteria, kefir is a great way to keep your digestive system happy and healthy.
2. Kefir's unique combination of vitamins and nutrients has been shown to help calm the nervous system.
3. The antioxidants in kefir have been shown to help improve skin condition, including reducing acne, psoriasis, and wrinkles.

HEALTH BENEFITS

Kefir has many of the same qualities and benefits of another probiotic superstar—yogurt—but it's created in a different way. Kefir contains more than 30 different probiotic cultures and healthy bacteria that can help alleviate many intestinal issues, as well as help rebuild the healthy intestinal bacteria of people who have been on antibiotics or suffered from serious illness.

Its particular combination of vitamins and minerals has a relaxing effect on our nervous system. A diet rich in kefir has also been shown to help alleviate some of the symptoms of anxiety, sleep disorders, depression, and ADHD.

The combination of antioxidants found in kefir has been shown to help keep skin happy and healthy—even helping to prevent acne, reduce psoriasis outbreaks, and prevent wrinkles.

AVAILABILITY

Kefir has made its way from being found strictly at health food stores to being available in many supermarket dairy cases. You can find both sweetened and flavored kefir (often in many of the same flavors as yogurt) and plain kefir. To control the sugar and additives in your kefir, try buying plain and blending in your own fruit and sweeteners in a blender.

You can also make your own kefir! Kefir is made by placing kefir grains (yeast cultures) in milk and letting the mixture ferment at room temperature for a certain period of time. You can find kefir grains at major health food stores and online. If you take care of your kefir grains, you'll never need to buy them again and always have a fresh supply of kefir (for a lot cheaper than they sell the beverage in stores).

HOW TO USE

Kefir is somewhere between the thickness of whole milk and that of yogurt, making it a great base for smoothies and Popsicles, and even a thick and creamy addition to cereals instead of using milk. The flavor of kefir also makes it a great substitute for buttermilk in cooking and baking. Some folks enjoy just drinking kefir plain, or mixed with fruit and sweetener.

MILLET

Yup, this is the same millet that you'll find in birdseed, but millet isn't just for the birds. This gluten-free whole grain cooks up fluffy and flavorful and is a favorite of many health food experts.

QUICK FACTS

1. Millet is a great source of magnesium, a mineral that is deficient in many diets.
2. Like many other whole grains, millet is an excellent option for its cancer-fighting and heart-helping benefits.
3. Millet can be used in place of oatmeal for a change of pace at the breakfast table.

HEALTH BENEFITS

Studies have shown that at least half of people eating a modern diet are deficient in magnesium—a deficiency that can lead to muscle spasms and cramps, headaches, and even seizures or abnormal heart rhythms. Millet is a good source of magnesium, and in particular, has been shown to help reduce the frequency and severity of migraines, and lower high blood pressure and the risk of heart attack.

As with many other whole grains, a diet rich in millet can significantly lower the risk of type 2 diabetes and asthma, help prevent heart failure and gallstones, and help protect against cancer.

AVAILABILITY

You don't have to browse the pet food aisle to find millet; it's available in the bulk bins and grain sections of most health food stores and some larger supermarkets.

HOW TO USE

Cook millet as you would rice or any whole grain, in a ratio of two and a half parts liquid to one part millet. Use it as a healthy side dish or as part of pilafs and salads. You can also use millet as a substitute for oatmeal or other hot breakfast cereals.

MILLET TABBOULEH

Typically, tabbouleh is made using bulgur wheat, which is an amazing whole grain but can take a bit of getting used to for folks who don't enjoy whole grains. Here, I sub in gluten-free millet, which cooks up fluffy and soft. The millet absorbs the simple lemon–olive oil dressing beautifully and the flavors of this salad just keep getting better and better as it chills.

MAKES: *8 servings*
TIME: *30 minutes (plus chilling time)*

1 cup millet

2 ½ cups chicken or vegetable broth

Juice of 2 lemons

¼ cup extra-virgin olive oil

1 bunch green onions, pale green and white parts only, sliced

½ cup minced fresh mint

1 cup minced fresh parsley

1 large cucumber, peeled, seeded, and diced

2 cups cherry tomatoes, halved

Salt and pepper

Place the millet and broth in a medium-size saucepan, bring to a boil over medium-high heat, lower the heat to low, cover, and simmer for 20 to 25 minutes, or until the liquid has been absorbed. Remove from the heat and let rest, covered, for 10 minutes. Meanwhile, stir together the lemon juice, olive oil, green onions, mint, parsley, cucumber, and cherry tomatoes in a large bowl. Add the millet and stir to combine. Season liberally with salt and pepper to taste. Refrigerate until the salad is cold, about an hour.

NUTRITION PER SERVING: 184 CALORIES, 8.1 G FAT, 23.3 G CARBS, 5.5 G PROTEIN

THIS SALAD IS AN EXCELLENT SIDE DISH FOR BAKED FALAFEL LETTUCE WRAPS WITH TAHINI-YOGURT SAUCE (PAGE 112).

GREEK QUINOA SALAD

This cold grain salad has an incredible combination of sweet and salty flavors that evokes the feeling of sitting on a Mediterranean beach.

MAKES: 8 servings
TIME: 50 minutes

1 cup quinoa, rinsed

1 ½ cups vegetable broth

1 medium-size cucumber, peeled, seeded, and diced

8 ounces grape tomatoes, halved

1 medium-size red bell pepper, seeded and diced

1 loose cup fresh parsley, minced

½ red onion, diced

1 cup kalamata olives, halved

4 ounces feta cheese, crumbled or cubed

¼ cup extra-virgin olive oil

¼ cup red wine vinegar

½ teaspoon dried oregano

1 teaspoon fresh dill

½ teaspoon kosher salt

½ teaspoon ground black pepper

1 teaspoon honey

1 teaspoon lemon juice

In a medium-size saucepan, stir together the quinoa and broth. Bring to a boil over high heat, stir once, lower the heat to low, cover, and cook for 20 to 25 minutes, or until the liquid is absorbed. Remove from the heat and let rest for 5 minutes. Fluff with a fork. In a large mixing bowl, combine the cooked quinoa, cucumber, tomatoes, red pepper, parsley, onion, olives, and feta. In a small bowl, combine the olive oil, red wine vinegar, oregano, dill, salt, pepper, honey, and lemon juice. Pour over the salad and stir to combine. Refrigerate for at least an hour to allow the flavors to meld.

NUTRITION PER SERVING: 201 CALORIES, 10.2 G FAT, 19.1 G CARBS, 9.2 G PROTEIN

THIS SALAD IS A GREAT, BALANCED,
ONE-BOWL MEAL FOR LUNCHES.
MAKE UP A BIG BATCH OF IT ON THE
WEEKEND AND DOLE IT OUT ALL
WEEK LONG.

STRAWBERRY-CHICKEN SPINACH WRAPS

Wraps are one of my favorite foods to eat for lunches—they're like the best parts of both a salad and a sandwich. This wrap is packed with a ton of different flavors and textures that blend together beautifully. No tortillas kicking around? No problem, just toss the filling into a bowl and eat it salad style.

I LIKE TO ROAST A WHOLE CHICKEN ON THE WEEKEND, AND THEN USE THE LEFTOVERS FOR RECIPES (SUCH AS THESE WRAPS) ALL WEEK LONG.

MAKES: 4 servings
TIME: 15 minutes

For the dressing

½ cup sliced, hulled strawberries

Juice and zest of 1 lime

¼ cup balsamic vinegar

⅓ cup extra-virgin olive oil

1 tablespoon honey

2 teaspoons Dijon mustard

½ teaspoon salt

For the wraps

4 large whole wheat flour tortillas

8 cups baby spinach

8 ounces sliced, cooked chicken breast

4 ounces crumbled feta cheese

½ medium-size cucumber, sliced thinly

1 avocado, pitted, peeled, and cut into slices

½ cup sliced, hulled strawberries

3 green onions, sliced thinly

To prepare the dressing, combine all the dressing ingredients in a blender. Blend on high speed until emulsified—about 30 seconds. Set aside.

To prepare each wrap, lay out one tortilla, then pile on one-quarter of the spinach, chicken breast, feta, cucumber, avocado, strawberries, and green onions. Drizzle with some of the dressing. Roll the wrap tightly, slice in half, and serve.

NUTRITION PER SERVING: 510 CALORIES, 27.7 G FAT, 40.2 G CARBS, 29.7 G PROTEIN

ROASTED VEGGIE & BLACK BEAN RICE BOWLS

The slow-roasted veggies in these bowls makes them so incredibly flavorful that you'll never miss the meat. Top these bowls with your favorite taco toppings—sour cream, avocado, chopped cilantro—whatever makes you happy!

MAKES: 8 servings
TIME: 40 minutes

Cooking spray

1 tablespoon olive oil

2 cloves garlic, minced

1 teaspoon ground cumin

1 tablespoon chili powder

Salt and pepper

2 medium-size sweet potatoes, diced

1 medium-size red onion, diced

1 large red bell pepper, seeded and diced

1 jalapeño pepper, seeded and chopped finely

3 cups cooked brown rice

2 14-ounce cans black beans, drained and rinsed

Lime wedges

Toppings (avocado, chopped cilantro, sour cream, cheese, etc.)

Preheat the oven to 400°F. Spray a baking sheet with cooking spray; set aside. In a medium-size bowl, mix together the olive oil, garlic, cumin, chili powder, and salt and pepper to taste until combined. Add the sweet potatoes, onions, red peppers, and jalapeño and toss to coat. Spread out the veggies in a single layer on the prepared baking sheet. Roast for 20 to 30 minutes, stirring occasionally, until the veggies are tender and beginning to brown and caramelize.

To assemble the bowls, spoon rice into each bowl and top with black beans, then with roasted veggies. Spritz the bowl with lime juice and then top with your desired toppings.

NUTRITION PER SERVING (NOT INCLUDING TOPPINGS): 385 CALORIES, 4 G FAT, 73 G CARBS, 17 G PROTEIN

FOR EACH SERVING OF THIS DISH,
YOU GET 112 PERCENT OF YOUR
RECOMMENDED DAILY ALLOWANCE
OF VITAMIN A, WHICH IS VITAL FOR
KEEPING YOUR EYES, SKIN, BONES,
AND IMMUNE SYSTEM HEALTHY.

RAINBOW TOMATO & BASIL SALAD

This recipe may seem too simple to be delicious, but it's really out-of-this-world flavorful! Make sure you only make this when you can get your hands on the freshest tomatoes available—your taste buds will thank you for waiting until the middle of summer.

MAKES: 4 servings
TIME: 5 minutes

3 cups chopped tomatoes
(in various colors and sizes)

¼ cup chiffonaded fresh basil

2 tablespoons extra-virgin olive oil

1 tablespoon balsamic vinegar

Salt and pepper

In a medium-size bowl, toss together the tomatoes and basil until well combined. Drizzle with the olive oil and vinegar. Season with salt and pepper to taste.

NUTRITION PER SERVING: 81 CALORIES, 7.2 G FAT, 4.5 G CARBS, 1.1 G PROTEIN

YOU CAN QUICKLY TURN THIS INTO A WELL-ROUNDED LUNCH SALAD BY TOSSING IN SOME CRUMBLED FETA OR FRESH MOZZARELLA CHUNKS, AND SERVING IT WITH A PIECE OF CRUSTY BREAD FOR SOPPING UP THE DELICIOUS DRESSING.

BAKED FALAFEL LETTUCE WRAPS

with Tahini-Yogurt Sauce

Standard falafel sandwiches have deep-fried chickpea balls wrapped in fluffy pita bread—this version is a healthier, lighter baked version, but with all the flavor of the original!

THIS ALSO MAKES AN AWESOME DIPPING SAUCE FOR VEGGIES AND CHIPS!

MAKES: 4 servings
TIME: 1 hour

For the tahini sauce

1 clove garlic

½ teaspoon kosher salt

¼ cup tahini

2 tablespoons lemon juice

Pinch of ground black pepper

¼ cup plain yogurt

For the falafel patties

Cooking spray

2 cups cooked chickpeas (about 1 14-ounce can)

1 small onion, chopped roughly

2 cloves garlic

1 large egg

2 teaspoons ground cumin

1 teaspoon kosher salt

1 teaspoon lemon juice

1 teaspoon baking powder

½ cup whole wheat panko bread crumbs

½ teaspoon ground black pepper

For the wraps

Leaves of Bibb or iceberg lettuce

Cucumber slices

Tomato slices

Minced fresh parsley

To prepare the tahini sauce, mash together the garlic clove and kosher salt with a mortar and pestle or the back of a spoon until it turns into a paste. In a small bowl, whisk together the garlic mash, tahini, lemon juice, ground pepper, and yogurt until it's a drizzle-able consistency. Set aside.

To prepare the falafel patties, preheat the oven to 400°F and spray a baking sheet with cooking spray. Pulse together the chickpeas, onion, and garlic in a food processor until well chopped. Add the egg, cumin, salt, lemon juice, baking soda, bread crumbs, and ground pepper. Pulse until just combined. Form the chickpea mixture into 15 balls or patties and arrange on the prepared baking sheet. Spray the tops of the balls with cooking spray. Bake for 15 to 20 minutes, or until the tops are golden brown and begin to split.

To assemble the lettuce wraps, layer the cucumber and tomato slices on lettuce leaves, top with the falafel, and drizzle with tahini sauce. Sprinkle with parsley before serving.

NUTRITION PER SERVING: 554 CALORIES, 16.6 G FAT, 78.7 G CARBS, 26.5 G PROTEIN

3

DINNER

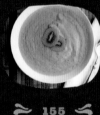

155   126   148   144

ALMOND-CRUSTED CHICKEN

These oven-baked chicken strips are a great take-out-fake-out version of the deep-fried chicken you'll find at many fast-food restaurants. The almond breading keeps the chicken moist and tender while crisping up in the oven.

MAKES: 4 servings
TIME: 45 minutes

1 cup almonds

1 tablespoon paprika

1 teaspoon garlic powder

¼ teaspoon cayenne pepper

½ teaspoon ground black pepper

1 teaspoon salt

2 large eggs

2 tablespoons milk

1 pound boneless, skinless chicken breasts, cut into 1-inch strips

Cooking spray

Preheat the oven to 375°F. Pulse the almonds in a food processor until crushed into small crumbs. Add the paprika, garlic powder, cayenne, ground pepper, and salt. Pulse again to just mix. Transfer the almond mixture to a shallow baking dish. In a second baking dish, whisk together the eggs and milk. Dredge a chicken strip in the egg mixture, and then press into the almond mixture until well coated on both sides. Gently transfer the chicken to a baking sheet. Repeat with the remaining chicken strips. Spray the tops of the chicken strips with cooking spray and bake for 15 to 20 minutes, or until the crust is crisp.

NUTRITION PER SERVING: 398 CALORIES, 23.0 G FAT, 7.3 G CARBS, 41.3 G PROTEIN

FOR AN EXTRA BOOST OF SUPERFOODS, SERVE THESE STRIPS WITH HONEY MUSTARD FOR DIPPING. JUST MIX TOGETHER EQUAL PARTS MUSTARD, HONEY, AND KEFIR.

ALMONDS

Almonds are probably nothing new to your kitchen, but once you learn how super they really are, you might start using them more frequently. We like to think of almonds as nuts, but they're technically the seed of a fruit! Whatever you call them, they're delicious, versatile, and crazy good for you.

QUICK FACTS

❶ High-calorie, high-fat, high-protein almonds are a terrific quick energy boost on the go.
❷ Almonds are packed with healthy fats that may help reduce the risk of heart disease.
❸ Almonds are a good source of many trace minerals that are lacking in most diets.

HEALTH BENEFITS

Almonds are a high-fat food—but not all fats are created equal. The monounsaturated fats found in almonds have been shown to help reduce the risk of heart disease and lower "bad" cholesterol. Almonds are also a great source of a few minerals that are commonly lacking in our diets. Grab a handful or two of raw almonds to get your fill of riboflavin (a.k.a. vitamin B2), manganese, and copper—trace nutrients that can help keep your energy levels up.

AVAILABILITY

Today there are thousands of almond products on store shelves, but for the best health benefits, grab raw, unsalted almonds. If you prefer the taste of roasted almonds, look for "dry-roasted" versions (those haven't been roasted in oil) or toast them at home in your oven.

HOW TO USE

Almonds can be eaten alone, stirred into a healthy trail mix, or incorporated into healthy cooking or baking. They're very versatile! To bring out the nutty, warm flavor of almonds, toast them at home in a preheated 200°F oven for 15 to 20 minutes. This helps preserve the delicate fatty compounds in the nuts, while still imparting a roasted flavor.

AVOCADOS

It's hard to beat a perfectly seasoned bowl of fresh guacamole and a pile of warm tortilla chips! But did you know that the benefits of avocados go way beyond being a base for your favorite chip dip?

QUICK FACTS

1 Avocados are packed with healthy fats and other compounds that are naturally anti-inflammatory.

2 Avocados have been shown to help reduce the risk of many cancers, including cancers of the mouth, skin, and prostate.

3 The high fat and protein levels in avocados help you feel fuller longer.

HEALTH BENEFITS

Most fruits and veggies are low-fat foods, but avocados are packed with healthy fats. Don't fear the fat! The fats in avocados have been shown to help curb inflammatory diseases, such as arthritis; help us absorb our nutrients; and lower our risk of heart disease. A diet rich in avocados has also been shown to help reduce the risk of cancer (specifically, cancers of the mouth, skin, and prostate) as well as regulate blood sugar and help prevent and control diabetes.

AVAILABILITY

Nowadays you'd be hard-pressed to find a supermarket without a well-stocked avocado section. Ripe avocados are firm, but have a slight give when squeezed lightly.

HOW TO USE

To get the most health benefits from an avocado, make sure you get all the dark green flesh next to the peel (use a spoon to scoop it out). Avocados are best eaten raw—use them chopped or sliced in salads or mash them to make a great substitute for mayo on sandwiches.

NUTRITION HIGHLIGHTS PER 1 AVOCADO

232	21g	12g	3g	40%	24%	20%
CALORIES	FAT	CARBS	PROTEIN	DIETARY FIBER	VITAMIN C	VITAMIN B6

GRILLED CHICKEN GUACAMOLE TOSTADAS

Guacamole can be used for so much more than just a chip dip!
These tostadas use creamy, cool guacamole as a spread—
it's great paired with the spicy salsa and smoky chicken.

THESE TOSTADAS ARE ALSO GREAT WITH GRILLED SHRIMP, STEAK, OR PORTOBELLO MUSHROOMS.

MAKES: 4 servings
TIME: 35 minutes

For the guacamole

2 ripe avocados, pitted, scooped from skin, and mashed

½ medium-size onion, diced

2 plum tomatoes, diced

¼ cup fresh cilantro, minced

1 clove garlic, minced

Juice of 1 lime

Salt and pepper

For the salsa

½ medium-size onion, diced

3 plum tomatoes, diced

¼ cup fresh cilantro, minced

1 jalapeño pepper, seeds and membranes removed, minced

1 clove garlic, minced

Juice of 1 lime

Salt and pepper

For the tostadas

2 chicken breasts

2 tablespoons olive oil

Juice and zest of 1 lime

1 tablespoon ground cumin

8 small whole-grain tortillas

Your choice of toppings
(Monterey Jack cheese, sour cream, etc.)

Preheat the grill to medium-high heat.

To prepare the guacamole, combine all the guacamole ingredients in a bowl; set aside.

To prepare the salsa, combine all the salsa ingredients in a separate bowl; set aside.

To prepare the chicken, toss the chicken breasts with the olive oil, lime juice and zest, and cumin. Grill for 10 minutes on each side, or until cooked through. Remove from the heat and shred the meat. Place the tortillas on the grill, and cook for about a minute per side, or until just crisp and browned. Assemble the tostadas by spreading the guacamole on each tortilla, topping with the chicken, salsa, and other desired toppings.

NUTRITION PER SERVING (NOT INCLUDING EXTRA TOPPINGS): 600 CALORIES, 35.7 G FAT, 46.5 G CARBS, 29.5 G PROTEIN

BEEF & BARLEY STEW

It's hard to beat the classic combination of beef and barley!
Serve this up on a cool fall day with a big hunk of crusty,
whole-grain bread.

MAKES: *8 servings*
TIME: *1 hour*

2 tablespoons olive oil, divided

¼ cup white whole wheat flour

2 pounds beef stew meat,
cut into ½-inch pieces

1 large onion, diced

4 large carrots, sliced into thick rounds

4 large stalks celery, diced

2 cloves garlic, minced

12 ounces button mushrooms, sliced

1 (14 ½-ounce) can stewed tomatoes

1 cup dry red wine

4 cups beef broth

2 bay leaves

¾ teaspoon dried thyme

Salt and pepper

1 cup uncooked barley

In a large soup pot, heat 1 tablespoon of the
olive oil over medium-high heat until hot.
While the pot is heating, toss the meat with
the flour and shake off any extra. Add to the
pot and sear on all sides until just browned.
Remove the meat from the pot and set aside.
Add the remaining tablespoon of olive oil to
the pot and heat. Add the onion, carrots, celery,
and garlic and cook until just softened, about
8 minutes. Add the mushrooms, tomatoes,
red wine, broth, bay leaves, thyme, and salt
and pepper to taste. Scrape the bottom of
the pot to release all the deliciousness left
from searing the meat. Add back the meat.
Bring to a boil, and add the barley. Lower
the heat, cover, and simmer for 45 minutes
to an hour, or until the barley is cooked and
the meat is tender. Remove the bay leaves
before serving.

NUTRITION PER SERVING: 434 CALORIES,
12.1 G FAT, 32.2 G CARBS, 42.8 G PROTEIN

*IF YOU USED HULLED BARLEY INSTEAD OF
PEARLED, THIS STEW MAY TAKE A BIT LONGER
TO SIMMER AND REQUIRE A BIT MORE BROTH TO
GET THE BARLEY TENDER.*

BARLEY

The flavor and texture of barley make it one of the kitchen's most versatile whole grains. It's mild-flavored, nutty, and has a chew that resembles that of pasta.

QUICK FACTS

1 The dietary fiber in barley is known to help reduce the risk of cardiovascular and intestinal diseases.

2 Barley has been shown to help lower the risk of type 2 diabetes, and help control diabetes in those who already have the disease.

3 The high fiber and selenium levels in barley combine to help reduce the risk of colon cancer.

HEALTH BENEFITS

Like a lot of whole grains, barley is a dietary fiber superstar. Studies have shown that people with diets rich in barley have a reduced risk of colon and many other forms of cancer, hemorrhoids, and gallstones—thanks to the high-quality fiber. They also lower cholesterol numbers. Barley is a particularly powerful ally for postmenopausal women, helping lower their risk of cardiovascular disease.

AVAILABILITY

It might be easy to miss, but many grocery stores carry barley in their rice section. Also, check for affordable barley in the bulk section of many stores. You might see three different kinds of barley—pearled, hulled, and flaked. Hulled barley is the least processed version, but pearled barley is the most common form, and still retains most of barley's nutritional benefits.

HOW TO USE

Barley cooks up just like rice, quinoa, and other whole grains. Cook it in water or broth for a tasty whole-grain side dish, or add it to soups and stews for a nice whole-grain burst of texture and nutrition.

BEETS

A lot of folks turn up their noses when you mention eating beets, but the earthy, sweet flavor of beets and their rich color make them a superfood you shouldn't skip.

QUICK FACTS

❶ Beets contain a unique combination of antioxidants that help reduce the risk of many inflammatory diseases.

❷ The betalins in beets help the body's cells with detoxification.

❸ Their high concentration of antioxidants makes beets a powerful anticancer food.

❹ The specific type of fiber in beets may provide special health benefits to the digestive tract.

HEALTH BENEFITS

Beets are packed with a unique combination of phytonutrients that function as both antioxidants and anti-inflammatories. These compounds (found in both golden and purple beets) may help lower the risk of heart disease and reduce the effects of diabetes. Beets are packed with betalins, compounds that help the body's cells detoxify.

AVAILABILITY

Beets are at their freshest and sweetest during the cooler weather months, and can be found in most grocery stores and farmers' markets during the fall and winter. The smaller the beet, the sweeter and milder the flavor, so opt for small, tender beets if you're beet shy.

HOW TO USE

The healthy compounds in beets break down rapidly the longer they are cooked, so for best nutrition cook them until they are just fork tender, by either roasting or steaming.

BEET & BLACK BEAN BURGERS

I'm the first to admit that these burgers aren't a quick or simple recipe. But I promise they're worth the work! The slow-roasted vegetables and combo of flavors and textures make these some of the best vegetarian burgers on the block. You can serve these to veg-heads and carnivores alike, and I promise they'll both be satisfied.

MAKES: 8 large burgers
TIME: 1 hour 30 minutes

3 large beets, scrubbed and greens removed

1 large onion, chopped roughly

3 cloves garlic, chopped roughly

2 tablespoons olive oil

2 cups cooked brown rice

2 tablespoons cider vinegar

1 cup rolled oats

3 cups cooked black beans

½ cup unsweetened applesauce

1 tablespoons paprika

1 tablespoon dry mustard

1 teaspoon ground cumin

1 tablespoon Worcestershire sauce

1 large egg

½ teaspoon salt

½ teaspoon ground black pepper

Olive oil (if panfrying)

Whole wheat hamburger buns
and burger toppings

MAKE THE MOST OF YOUR TIME:
THESE BURGERS FREEZE BEAUTIFULLY.
YOU CAN DOUBLE OR TRIPLE THE RECIPE,
AND FREEZE THEM FLAT BEFORE THE
FINAL COOKING STEP. ONCE FROZEN,
TRANSFER TO A RESEALABLE PLASTIC
FREEZER BAG FOR LONG-TERM STORAGE.
JUST THAW BEFORE COOKING, THEN
FOLLOW THE REMAINDER OF THE RECIPE.

Preheat the oven to 350°F. Wrap each of the beets tightly in aluminum foil. Place in a small baking dish and bake for 40 to 50 minutes, or until fork tender. Let cool until the beets can be handled, then peel off the skins and discard. Shred the beets finely, and then place in a colander and press (using your fingers or a spoon) to squeeze out some of the liquid. Set the beets aside.

While the beets cook, toss the onion and garlic with the olive oil, spread the mixture in a single layer on a small baking sheet, and bake for 30 to 40 minutes, stirring occasionally, or until the onion has begun to brown and is very soft.

In a food processor, combine the shredded beets, onion mixture, and all the remaining ingredients except the olive oil, buns, and toppings. Pulse until the mixture comes together enough to form patties—adding more oats if necessary to keep the mixture together. Chill the mixture for at least 30 minutes, then form into eight large patties.

To pan-fry the burgers, heat a large, nonstick skillet with olive oil over medium-high heat. Add the burgers and cook for 5 minutes per side—or until the edges are browned and the burgers are warmed through. Serve on a bun with your favorite toppings.

To grill the burgers, preheat the grill to medium-high heat. Place the burgers on well-oiled grill grates and grill for about 4 minutes per side—or until the edges are browned and the burgers are warmed through. Serve on a bun with your favorite toppings.

NUTRITION PER BURGER (NOT INCLUDING BUN OR TOPPINGS): 253 CALORIES, 5.5 G FAT, 41.3 G CARBS, 11.0 G PROTEIN

GRILLED FISH TACOS
with Blueberry-Avocado Salsa

We've all heard how important it is to have a diet rich in healthy,
light, protein-packed fish. But the unfortunate thing is fish can
be really, totally, completely boring—especially when you're
working with some of the milder fish varieties, such as cod or tilapia.
One way to spice up eating fish: tacos! Fish tacos are super-flavorful,
totally fun, and crazy quick and easy to pull together. These are
a great way to spice up a ho-hum Tuesday night.

MAKES: 4 servings
TIME: 20 minutes (plus marinating time)

For the marinade

1 tablespoon ground cumin

1 teaspoon ground paprika

¼ cup chopped fresh cilantro

3 cloves garlic, smashed

Zest and juice of 1 lime

1 teaspoon salt

2 tablespoons coconut oil, melted

1 pound mild white fish
(cod or tilapia both work)

For the tacos

1 avocado, pitted, scooped from skin,
and diced

⅔ cup fresh blueberries, chopped roughly

¼ cup chopped fresh cilantro

1 jalapeño pepper, minced;
discard seeds and membranes
for a milder flavor

Zest and juice of 1 lime

Salt and pepper

12 corn tortillas

Lime wedges

To prepare the marinade, combine all the marinade ingredients, except the fish, in a large resealable plastic bag. Add the fish fillets, seal the bag, and gently turn to coat the fish. Let marinate in the fridge for at least 30 minutes, or up to overnight.

To prepare the tacos, preheat the grill to medium-high heat. In a medium-size bowl, mix together the avocado, blueberries, cilantro, jalapeño, lime juice and zest, and salt and pepper to taste. Set aside. Wrap the stack of tortillas in aluminum foil. Place the tortilla packet on the coolest part of the grill to warm while grilling the marinated fish on well-oiled grill grates (or on aluminum foil) until opaque and flaky, 7 to 10 minutes, depending on the thickness of the fish. Remove the fish and tortillas from the grill. To assemble the tacos, place one-twelfth of the fish in the center of a tortilla, top with one-twelfth of the blueberry mixture, and finish with a squeeze of fresh lime juice.

NUTRITION PER TACO SERVING:
403 CALORIES, 13.3 G FAT, 41.8 G CARBS,
31.6 G PROTEIN

TO MAKE THIS A SUPERFAST WEEKNIGHT DINNER, PREP THE MARINADE IN THE MORNING. NOT ONLY DOES IT STREAMLINE THE PROCESS, BUT IT ALSO GIVES THE FISH MAXIMUM TIME TO SOAK UP ALL THE YUMMY MARINADE FLAVOR.

BLUEBERRIES

You'd be hard-pressed to find someone who hasn't had a blueberry at least once. Blueberries are the second-most-popular berry (right behind strawberries), and for good reason. Not only are they incredibly delicious, but their health benefits make them one of the best options in the produce aisle.

QUICK FACTS

❶ Blueberries contain one of the highest amounts of antioxidants among any commonly consumed food.

❷ Blueberries are one of the few fruits native to North America.

❸ The wide range of antioxidants in blueberries helps strengthen nearly every single system in the body.

❹ Studies have shown blueberries help support healthy blood pressure levels, improve memory, balance blood sugar, protect the eyes from sun damage, and prevent cancer.

HEALTH BENEFITS

Most of the research regarding the healthy benefits of blueberries has focused on their antioxidant values. Many foods contain antioxidants, but what sets blueberries apart is their unique cocktail: The number and variety of antioxidants found in blueberries have been shown to benefit nearly every single organ and system in the human body. Most prominently, diets rich in blueberries have been shown to help with memory, cardiovascular health, blood sugar control, eye health, and cancer prevention (specifically those of the breast, colon, esophagus, and intestine).

AVAILABILITY

Both conventionally grown and organic fresh blueberries are available year-round in most supermarkets; however, if you're concerned about pesticide intake, make sure you stick with organic. Blueberries are listed in the top 12 worst crops for pesticide use if grown conventionally.

If fresh blueberries aren't available or are cost-prohibitive, frozen blueberries are a great option. Researchers have discovered that freezing blueberries does little to negatively impact their health benefits.

During the summertime, make sure to check around for fresh, local blueberries—they're one of the few fruits native to North America, and most regions can grow numerous varieties.

HOW TO USE

To get the most nutritional benefits from blueberries, keep them raw! Cooking berries over 350°F begins to deteriorate their nutritional benefits (although you still get some benefits).

85
CALORIE

RIES

19%
E VITAMIN C

GARLIC

We're all used to a heavy dose of garlic in our favorite Italian dishes, but the health benefits of garlic mean it deserves a spot in most of your savory dishes. Garlic isn't just a great flavor—it's a superfood!

QUICK FACTS

❶ Garlic is one of the best foods to consume if you're concerned about cardiovascular health.

❷ With natural antiviral and antibacterial properties, garlic can help your body fight off illness.

❸ The anti-inflammatory benefits of garlic apply to nearly all the systems of the body.

❹ The compounds in garlic stand up well to cooking, but for the maximum health benefits, eat garlic raw.

HEALTH BENEFITS

I could write an entire book on the health benefits of garlic (and in fact, there are many out there), but its health benefits basically boil down to garlic's sulfur compounds. These compounds are what give garlic its strong odor and flavor, but they are also the source of most of its health profits.

Garlic has been studied at length in regard to cardiovascular health. It has been shown to help regulate blood cholesterol and triglyceride levels, as well as help protect the blood cells and blood vessels. Garlic also helps keep clots from forming in our blood and lowers our blood pressure. If you want a healthy heart, eat a diet rich in garlic!

The anti-inflammatory benefits of garlic go way beyond just heart health, too. In fact, garlic has been shown to benefit our muscular, skeletal, and respiratory systems.

Garlic is also a natural antibacterial and antiviral, meaning it can help control the spread of bacteria and viruses in your body that may lead you to getting sick. Feel a cold coming on? Many folks swear that upping their raw garlic intake early during a cold helps shorten (or even completely stop) a cold.

AVAILABILITY

Fresh, raw garlic is available year-round in most supermarkets and farmers' markets. If you aren't a big fan of garlic, make sure you check out its different varieties. Garlic can range from spicy to mild, sweet to savory—there is a variety of garlic out there for almost every set of taste buds!

HOW TO USE

Garlic is used predominately cooked as an aromatic veggie addition to soups, casseroles, stews, and baked dishes. While the healthy compounds in garlic do tend to hold up well to cooking, to get the most benefit from garlic, you need to eat it raw! Try it blended in hummus or finely minced in salsa.

NUTRITION HIGHLIGHTS PER 1 CLOVE GARLIC

| 5 | 0g | 1g | 0.2g | 2% | 1% |

SHRIMP TACOS
with Red Cabbage Slaw

We all eat with our eyes, and these tacos do not disappoint our peepers! The red cabbage slaw makes a beautiful backdrop to perfectly seared shrimp. Bonus: This dinner is ready in less than half an hour.

YOU CAN ALSO PLACE THE SHRIMP ON PRESOAKED WOODEN SKEWERS AND GRILL THEM UNTIL JUST OPAQUE, ABOUT 5 MINUTES.

MAKES: *4 servings*
TIME: *20 minutes (plus marinating time)*

For the shrimp

1 tablespoon olive oil

1 teaspoon garlic powder

1 teaspoon ground cumin

1 teaspoon chili powder

½ teaspoon salt

1 pound raw shrimp

For the slaw

1 small head red cabbage, shredded

½ cup fresh cilantro, minced

2 green onions, sliced

½ teaspoon ground cumin

Zest and juice of 2 limes

½ teaspoon garlic powder

2 tablespoons cider vinegar

2 tablespoons honey

For the tacos

12 small corn tortillas

½ cup crumbled Cotija cheese

Lime wedges

To prepare the shrimp, combine all the shrimp ingredients in a resealable plastic bag, toss to coat the shrimp, and then let marinate for 30 minutes.

Meanwhile, prepare the slaw by combining all slaw ingredients in a bowl, tossing to coat.

To prepare the tacos, heat a skillet over medium-high heat, add the shrimp, and cook until pink and opaque, about 5 minutes. Assemble the tacos by placing a spoonful of the slaw on each tortilla, topping with a few shrimp and a sprinkle of Cotija cheese, and serving with lime wedges.

NUTRITION PER TACO SERVING:
492 CALORIES, 15.1 G FAT, 55.0 G CARBS, 38.9 G PROTEIN

COFFEE-CRUSTED RIB EYE STEAKS

These steaks are a special treat for coffee lovers and coffee haters alike. When seared in the pan, the coffee takes on an earthy, nutty flavor that complements the beef beautifully. It doesn't taste like "coffee," it just tastes rich and decadent.

MAKES: *4 servings*
TIME: *15 minutes*

2 (8-ounce) rib eye steaks

2 tablespoons finely ground coffee

1 teaspoon ground black pepper

1 teaspoon salt

1 tablespoon olive oil

1 tablespoon butter

Heat a heavy-bottomed skillet (I like cast iron) over high heat. Heat the olive oil and butter in the pan. In a small bowl, mix together the coffee, ground pepper, and salt. Spread the mixture onto all sides of the steaks, coating well. Place the steaks in the preheated skillet (they should sizzle when you place them in; if not, your pan isn't hot enough) and cook on each side for 3 to 4 minutes to achieve medium-rare results. Let the steaks rest for at least 5 minutes before serving.

NUTRITION PER SERVING: 212 CALORIES, 12.4 G FAT, 0.3 G CARBS, 25.1 G PROTEIN

FOUR OUNCES OF STEAK MIGHT SEEM LIKE A SMALL SERVING SIZE, BUT REMEMBER, MOST HEALTH ORGANIZATIONS RECOMMEND YOU LIMIT YOUR RED MEAT INTAKE TO ONE TO TWO 4-OUNCE SERVINGS PER WEEK.

COFFEE

For a lot of us, we don't need any convincing to consume coffee, but if you're on the fence about a cup of morning joe, the health benefits of coffee should tip you onto the coffee-loving side.

QUICK FACTS

1 Regular coffee consumption may help reduce risk of neurodegenerative diseases.

2 Caffeine is a stimulant that helps you stay awake, but it also helps the connections in your brain happen more quickly.

3 Coffee is packed with trace amounts of vitamins, minerals, and antioxidants.

HEALTH BENEFITS

Your favorite benefit of the caffeine in coffee might be the pep in your step, but moderate consumption of caffeine also has some serious health benefits. It helps block a compound in your brain that slows the connections between neurotransmitters, making your memory clearer, your mood better, and your brain function better. There are also studies that show regular consumption of coffee might help protect you from neurodegenerative diseases, such as Alzheimer's, Parkinson's, and dementia.

While it may be tempting to think that coffee is just flavored water, it isn't! Coffee is packed with vitamins, minerals, and antioxidants that are present in the beans, and get passed into the final drink, too. In fact, coffee is one of the most common sources of antioxidants in the North American diet. The key to getting the health benefits of coffee: Consume in moderation.

AVAILABILITY

Brewed coffee is available at many shops in every city, and coffee beans and grounds are sold by every grocery store in your area. For the best flavor and nutrition, buy whole-bean coffee and grind it yourself.

HOW TO USE

You probably know how to brew a cup of coffee, but when it comes to cooking with coffee, you want the freshest beans you can find. The intricacies of the bean flavor really transfer to the final dish.

FARRO

Farro is a well-loved grain in Italy that has recently made a big impact here in North America, and for good reason! Farro has a nutty flavor and chewy texture that is incredibly hearty and delicious.

QUICK FACTS

1. Farro is a great source of heart-healthy whole-grain fiber.
2. The chewy texture of farro makes it work well in dishes in place of rice or pasta.
3. This grain is a good source of magnesium, which may help reduce tension and keep the vascular system healthy.
4. Farro has a special type of carbohydrate that has been shown to help strengthen the immune system.

HEALTH BENEFITS

Clocking it at eight grams per cup, farro is an impressive source of whole-grain fiber (that's nearly four times as much as white rice). A diet rich in whole-grain fiber has been shown to help lower cholesterol and keep our hearts healthy.

Farro isn't just about fiber, though; this grain is also an excellent source of magnesium, which has been shown to help relieve tension and help keep our vascular systems healthy.

If you're feeling a little under the weather, farro might be a good option to add to your pot of chicken soup. Farro has a unique type of carbohydrate that has been shown to help boost the immune system.

AVAILABILITY

Farro was nearly impossible to find in the regular grocery store a few years ago, but is now available in the whole-grain sections of many of the larger supermarkets. Farro is also available readily at Italian markets and delis, as well as in health food stores.

HOW TO USE

Farro cooks up just like rice or pasta (with a ratio of one part farro to two parts liquid), and in fact, is a great substitute for specialty rices, such as Arborio rice, for risotto. Cooked farro can be used in grain-based salads and side dishes, such as pilaf.

NUTRITION HIGHLIGHTS PER 1 CUP COOKED FARRO

170	1.5g	34g	6g	20%	15%	15%
CALORIES	FAT	CARBS	PROTEIN	NIACIN	MAGNESIUM	ZINC

CHEESY BAKED FARRO & CAULIFLOWER

This dish is one of my favorite ways to use my favorite veggie! If you're craving macaroni and cheese, but aren't 100 percent ready to dive headfirst into a bucket of refined carbs, this casserole is a great substitute. Chewy, hearty, whole-grain farro is mixed with tender cauliflower florets and then smothered in a gooey cheese sauce made with skim milk.

YOU CAN ALSO SERVE THIS MAC AND CHEESE SUBSTITUTE AS A SIDE DISH; IT'LL SERVE SIX TO EIGHT AS A SIDE.

MAKES: 4 main dish servings
TIME: 50 minutes

1 cup farro

2 cups vegetable broth

1 head cauliflower, cut into bite-size pieces

2 tablespoons butter

1 small onion, diced

1 clove garlic, minced

2 tablespoons white whole wheat flour

2 cups skim milk

½ cup freshly shredded Fontina cheese

½ cup freshly shredded sharp Cheddar cheese

Salt and pepper

½ cup whole wheat panko bread crumbs

Preheat the oven to 350°F. In a medium-size saucepan, combine the farro and broth over medium-high heat. Bring to a boil, lower the heat, and simmer until the liquid is absorbed and the farro is tender, about 10 minutes. Set aside. Meanwhile, bring a large pot full of water to a boil, add the cauliflower florets, and cook until fork tender, but not mushy, about 5 minutes. Drain and set aside.

While the farro and cauliflower are cooking, melt the butter in a small saucepan over medium heat. Add the onion and garlic and cook until tender, about 5 minutes. Whisk in the flour and continue to whisk constantly for 2 minutes. Slowly pour in the skim milk while whisking. Bring to a simmer and cook until thickened enough to coat the back of a spoon, about 7 minutes. Remove from the heat and whisk in the cheeses, and salt and pepper to taste.

To assemble the casserole, stir together the farro, cauliflower, and cheese sauce until everything is well coated. Pour into a casserole dish and then sprinkle the top with the bread crumbs. Cover with aluminum foil. Bake for 30 minutes, removing the foil during the last 10 minutes to brown the bread crumbs.

NUTRITION PER SERVING: 499 CALORIES, 15 G FAT, 57 G CARBS, 24 G PROTEIN

FARRO-STUFFED MINI PEPPERS

Mini sweet peppers are a great option for stuffing. Unlike regular stuffed peppers, the mini version gives you a lot more sweet pepper flavor in every bite.

IF YOU'RE HAVING A HARD TIME TRACKING DOWN MINI PEPPERS, YOU CAN ALSO STUFF REGULAR YELLOW OR RED BELL PEPPERS. JUST ADD 20 TO 30 MINUTES TO THE COOKING TIME.

MAKES: 6 servings
TIME: 50 minutes

½ cup farro

1 cup chicken broth

½ pound lean ground beef

1 tablespoon olive oil

Pinch of red pepper flakes

1 small onion, chopped

3 cloves garlic, minced

1 large tomato, diced

1 teaspoon dried oregano

1 teaspoon dried basil

1 teaspoon dried parsley

Salt and pepper

12 to 16 mini bell peppers (depending on size)

½ cup low-fat ricotta cheese

1 cup marinara sauce

½ cup low-fat mozzarella cheese

Preheat the oven to 350°F. In a medium-size saucepan, combine the farro and broth. Bring to a boil over high heat. Lower the heat to low, cover, and simmer for 10 to 12 minutes, or until the farro has absorbed all the liquid. Remove from the heat and let rest, covered, for 5 minutes. Fluff with a fork.

Meanwhile, in a large skillet, brown the beef over medium-high heat until cooked through. Remove the beef from the skillet and drain on paper towels. Return the skillet to the heat and add the olive oil and red pepper flakes. Cook for about 1 minute, or until the oil starts to shimmer. Add the onion and garlic and cook until tender, about 4 minutes. Then add the tomato, oregano, basil, parsley, salt and pepper to taste, and the cooked ground beef. Bring to a boil, lower the heat, and simmer for about 10 minutes, or until most of the liquid from the tomato is gone. Remove the mixture from the heat and stir in the cooked farro.

After scooping out ribs and seeds, begin to stuff the peppers by placing one spoonful of the beef mixture into the bottom of each mini pepper. Then "cap" the pepper with a small spoonful of the ricotta cheese. Once all the peppers are full, arrange them on their sides in a baking dish. Pour the marinara sauce over the top and sprinkle with the mozzarella. Bake for about 20 minutes, or until the cheese is brown and bubbly and the peppers are tender.

NUTRITION PER SERVING: 373 CALORIES, 19 G FAT, 32 G CARBS, 20 G PROTEIN

GREEK FREEKEH-STUFFED ZUCCHINI

These zucchini boats make a great side dish or,
thanks to the high protein and fiber content of freekeh,
a good option for a vegetarian main dish.

MAKES: 4 servings
TIME: 40 minutes

4 large zucchini

1 cup cooked freekeh

¼ cup fresh dill, minced

¼ cup fresh oregano, minced

1 small onion, diced

½ cup crumbled feta cheese

½ cup pitted kalamata olives, diced

1 tomato, diced

Salt and pepper

¼ cup whole wheat panko bread crumbs

2 tablespoons olive oil

*IF YOU HAVE ANY FILLING
LEFT OVER, PLACE IT IN A
SMALL BAKING DISH AND
BAKE ALONGSIDE THE
ZUCCHINI. IT MAKES FOR
A TASTY SIDE DISH!*

Preheat the oven to 375°F. Slice the zucchini in
half lengthwise, and using a spoon, scoop or
scrape out the inside of the halves, reserving
the flesh. Dice the zucchini flesh and mix with
the freekeh, dill, oregano, onion, feta, olives,
tomato, and salt and pepper to taste. Place the
zucchini halves on a baking sheet. Spoon the
mixture into the zucchini halves, mounding
them high. Sprinkle with the bread crumbs
and drizzle with the olive oil. Bake for 25 to
30 minutes, or until the zucchini is tender and
the bread crumbs are browned.

NUTRITION PER SERVING: 262 CALORIES,
14.4 G FAT, 29.5 G CARBS, 10.8 G PROTEIN

FREEKEH "MEAT" BALLS

We love noshing on freekeh as a side dish, but it also has the unique quality of being a really incredible vegetarian substitute for meat. It has a roasted, deep, nutty flavor that satisfies the same taste buds that crave meat, and a really nice "chew" that vegetarians and meat eaters alike enjoy. Here, I use freekeh as the base for some vegetarian "meat"balls. These are perfect with a big dollop of your favorite marinara sauce atop spaghetti.

THESE ALSO MAKE FOR A PRETTY GOOD VEGETARIAN "MEAT"BALL SUB!

MAKES: *6 servings*
TIME: *1 hour*

Cooking spray

2 ½ cups cooked freekeh

2 tablespoons olive oil

1 tablespoon lemon juice

⅓ cup rolled oats

½ cup whole wheat bread crumbs

½ cup grated Parmesan cheese

½ teaspoon salt

½ teaspoon ground black pepper

1 teaspoon balsamic vinegar

1 teaspoon paprika

1 teaspoon garlic powder

1 teaspoon onion powder

1 teaspoon dry mustard

1 teaspoon fresh parsley

1 large egg

Preheat the oven to 350°F. Coat a baking sheet with cooking spray; set aside. In a food processor, combine all the ingredients. Pulse until the mixture comes together to form a chunky paste (don't overmix). Using damp hands, form the mixture into sixteen 1 ½-inch balls and place on the prepared baking sheet. Spray the tops with cooking spray. Bake for 25 to 30 minutes, or until the balls are browned and crisp on the outside.

NUTRITION PER SERVING: 218 CALORIES, 10.9 G FAT, 21.0 G CARBS, 12.3 G PROTEIN

FREEKEH

A not-so-freaky food with a freaky name, freekeh (pronounced "free-kah") may be one of the whole grains in this book that you are unfamiliar with. Freekeh is an ancient grain that is made by roasting young, green wheat, giving it a nutty, smoky flavor.

QUICK FACTS

1 High levels of protein and fiber may help you maintain a healthy weight by keeping you feeling fuller longer.

2 Freekeh has high levels of two antioxidants that have been shown to promote eye health.

3 Freekeh is roasted from the young, green wheat plant, so it is not suitable for those with celiac disease or a wheat allergy.

HEALTH BENEFITS

Compared to its superfood grain counterparts, freekeh is one of the highest grain-based sources of both fiber and protein. This combination of macronutrients helps you feel fuller longer and consume smaller portion sizes, which may help you maintain a healthy weight.

Freekeh is also incredibly rich in the antioxidants lutein and zeaxanthin, two compounds that have been shown to promote eye health and help prevent macular degeneration.

AVAILABILITY

Freekeh can be a hard one to track down, but if you look in the whole-grain section of your local health food store, you might be able to find bags of it. It's also readily available from many health food retailers online.

HOW TO USE

Like other superfood grains, freekeh is prepared similarly to rice (using a two-to-one ratio of liquid to freekeh). Once the freekeh is cooked, it can be used in salads or side dishes. Freekeh also makes a great whole-grain addition to soups and stews.

NU   EKEH

260   8%

CALORIE   IRON

GRAPES

Grapes are one of the most ubiquitous fruits on the planet. They're cultivated on every continent except Antarctica, and have found their way into nearly every cuisine from every culture. Their prevalence is for good reason—these sweet, tart, and delicious little berries (yes, they are berries) are packed with a unique combination of nutrients that are incredibly good for us.

QUICK FACTS

1 Over 20 different phytonutrients found in grapes make them a powerful food to help all systems of the body.

2 Keep grapes at their freshest by only washing them immediately before you use them.

3 Exciting new research shows that grapes may be a powerful ally in the war against aging.

HEALTH BENEFITS

Depending on the variety, grapes can contain as many as 20 different phytonutrients.

Currently, research is being done to establish a connection between grapes and a healthy cardiovascular system, immune system, respiratory system, endocrine system, and nervous system. Promising research shows that grapes are a powerful anticancer food and is particularly effective against cancers of the colon, prostate, and breast.

Exciting research is also being done to observe the anti-aging benefits of a particular set of phytonutrients in grapes. Researchers have noted that people with diets rich in grapes not only live longer, but appear younger and even have better cognitive ability as they age.

AVAILABILITY

You'll be able to find numerous colors and varieties of table grapes at most supermarkets throughout the year. Fully ripe grapes have the highest concentration of antioxidants—they should appear plump and blemish free.

HOW TO USE

Grapes retain their nourishing benefits the best when eaten raw. However, cooking at 350°F or below will still keep available an impressive amount of antioxidants and nutrients.

Avoid washing or rinsing grapes until just before use. The white, dusty coating on grapes (called bloom) is actually a protective layer that helps keep grapes fresher, longer. Only clip off and wash what you need from the bunch each time.

NUTRITION HIGHLIGHTS PER 1 CUP GRAPES

62	0.3g	16g	0.6g	6%	5%	5%
CALORIES	FAT	CARBS	PROTEIN	VITAMIN C	VITAMIN B6	POTASSIUM

GRILLED CHICKEN, RED GRAPE & PESTO FLATBREAD PIZZAS

There is definitely a time and place for a rich, cheesy, topping-covered classic slice of pizza (with, hopefully, a pint of really great beer on the side), but this flatbread pizza is more fitting for eating outside on the porch with a glass of white wine on a warm summer evening. It's light, it's brightly flavored, and it won't leave you feeling as if you just ate your weight in grease and cheese. Plus, it's made on the grill, so no heating up your house with the oven!

MAKES: *8 servings*
TIME: *2 hours*

For the flatbreads

1 ½ cups warm water

½ teaspoon active dry yeast

4 cups white whole wheat flour, divided

1 teaspoon salt

2 tablespoons olive oil

For the pizzas

¼ cup olive oil

½ cup pesto

1 chicken breast, cooked and shredded

1 cup red grapes, halved

1 cup shredded Parmesan cheese

WANT TO TURN THIS INTO AN APPETIZER? JUST DIVIDE THE DOUGH INTO SMALL BALLS, AND BAKE UP MINI FLATBREADS INSTEAD OF A BIG ONE.

To prepare the flatbreads, mix the water and yeast in the bowl of a stand mixer or in a large mixing bowl. Let stand for 5 minutes, or until bubbly. Mix in 2 cups of the flour until well incorporated. Cover the bowl and let rise in a warm area for an hour. Once the rising time is over, add the remaining cup of flour and the salt and olive oil, and mix until well incorporated. Knead the dough (either by hand or using the dough hook of the stand mixer) for 5 to 7 minutes, or until smooth and stretchy. Transfer the dough to an oiled bowl, cover, and let rise for an additional 30 minutes. Punch down the dough and divide into four equal-size balls. Stretch out the balls to form flatbreads.

To prepare the pizzas, preheat the grill to medium-high heat. Oil the grates liberally. Working with two flatbreads at a time, place flat on the grill grates. Close the lid, and let cook for 3 to 5 minutes, or until the flatbreads begin to puff up and cook. Using a pastry brush, brush the olive oil on the uncooked side of the flatbreads, and then flip over, using tongs. Spread one-quarter of the pesto on each flatbread, followed by one-quarter of the chicken, one-quarter of the grapes, and one-quarter of the Parmesan. Close the grill lid and let cook for an additional 2 to 3 minutes, or until the cheese is melted. Remove the pizzas from the grill and repeat with the remaining two flatbreads.

NUTRITION PER FLATBREAD: 423 CALORIES, 17.7 G FAT, 50.8 G CARBS, 15.0 G PROTEIN

CREAMY CHICKEN & KALE ALFREDO

By using protein-packed, healthy Greek yogurt in place of heavy cream in this Alfredo sauce, you get a creamy, rich pasta sauce without a touch of guilt.

MAKES: 6 servings
TIME: 45 minutes

13 ounces whole wheat pasta

1 bunch kale, stems removed, torn into bite-size pieces

1 tablespoon butter

1 tablespoon olive oil

2 cloves garlic, minced

1 cup chicken broth

½ cup water

1 tablespoon arrowroot powder or cornstarch

¾ cup shredded Parmesan cheese, plus more for garnish

½ cup plain Greek yogurt

Salt and pepper

2 cups chopped cooked chicken

KALE IS GREAT IN THIS DISH BECAUSE IT RETAINS SOME OF ITS "CHEW" AND ADDS A REALLY INTERESTING TEXTURE TO THE PASTA. YOU COULD ALSO SUB IN FRESH SPINACH FOR A SIMILAR TASTE AND NUTRITIONAL BOOST.

Cook the pasta according to the package directions. Before draining, line a colander with the kale. Drain the pasta over the kale and return both the kale and the pasta to the cooking pot off the heat, reserving about ½ cup of the pasta-cooking water. The steam from the pasta will continue to wilt the kale. Set aside.

Meanwhile, while pasta is cooking, melt the butter and olive oil in a medium-size saucepan over medium heat. Add the garlic and cook until tender and fragrant, about 4 minutes. Add the chicken broth and bring to a boil.

In a small bowl, whisk together the water and arrowroot. Add the mixture to the chicken broth, lower the heat, and simmer for 5 to 7 minutes, or until the sauce is thickened. Turn off the heat, slide the pot over to a cool burner, and whisk in the ¾ cup of shredded Parmesan until melted. Let rest 5 minutes, then whisk in the Greek yogurt (if you do it before it's cooled down a little, the yogurt will turn grainy). Season to taste with salt and pepper.

Pour the sauce into the pot of pasta and kale and toss to coat, adding in some of the reserved pasta water if the mixture is too dry. Plate and top with the chopped chicken and additional shredded Parmesan.

NUTRITION PER SERVING: 443 CALORIES, 13.6 G FAT, 49.1 G CARBS, 31.4 G PROTEIN

KIWI IN SOUP? YUP! THE KIWI ADDS A TANGY SWEETNESS
TO THIS SOUP THAT IS OFF-THE-CHARTS DELICIOUS.

KIWI & SWEET POTATO BISQUE

Usually, *bisque* is a red-flag word meaning "full of cream, butter, and tons of other heavy ingredients," but this bisque is smooth, creamy, and 100 percent dairy free! It's a great option for serving to your vegan dinner guests.

MAKES: *8 servings*

TIME: *40 minutes*

2 tablespoons olive oil

3 cloves garlic, minced

1 large onion, diced

1 (½-inch) piece ginger, peeled and diced

3 large sweet potatoes, peeled and diced

6 cups vegetable broth

4 kiwis, peeled and roughly chopped

Salt and pepper

Heat the olive oil in a soup pot over medium-high heat. Add the garlic and onion and cook until tender and fragrant, about 5 minutes. Add the ginger, sweet potatoes, and broth. Bring to a boil, lower the heat, and simmer until the sweet potatoes are very tender, about 20 minutes. Remove from the heat, add the kiwis, and puree with an immersion blender until very smooth. Season with salt and pepper to taste.

NUTRITION PER SERVING: 224 CALORIES, 4.9 G FAT, 39.7 G CARBS, 6.0 G PROTEIN

KIWI

Kiwi (also known in some circles as the Chinese gooseberry)
is a small fruit with a texture and flavor all its own.
It originated in China, but has since been cultivated in
most of the warm climates across the globe.

QUICK FACTS

❶ Packed with more vitamin C than an orange, eating kiwi is a great way to help boost your immune system.

❷ Kiwi is a powerful protector from cell damage.

❸ Regular consumption of kiwi might help reduce the risk of many age-related eye disorders.

❹ Kiwi is a heart-healthy food that helps lower the risk of blood clots and regulate blood triglycerides.

HEALTH BENEFITS

You make think that citrus fruits cornered the vitamin C market, but kiwi is packed with even more vitamin C than an orange, making it one of the best foods to eat to help boost your immune system and shorten the length of colds.

The phytonutrients in kiwi are particularly exciting for their ability to protect DNA from damage. Studies have shown that, for children, a diet rich in kiwi may help the cells in their lungs and respiratory system develop healthier and stronger.

Kiwis are also important for their ability to protect our eyes. Studies have shown that eating a diet that includes three or more servings of fruit a day helps reduce the risk of age-related eye problems, such as macular degeneration.

Regular consumption of kiwi has also been shown to help lower the risk of blood clots and regulate blood triglycerides, making kiwi an important part of a heart-healthy diet.

AVAILABILITY

Kiwis were introduced to North America in the early 1960s as an exotic, tropical fruit, but are now prevalent enough to be found in most produce aisles. They grow the best in warm climates, but are available nearly year-round in most supermarkets.

HOW TO USE

Most people prefer to peel kiwi and eat the soft, green insides; however, the peel is edible (though a bit tough) and leaving it intact gives you more fiber and nutrients.

Kiwi should only be cut right before using. Not only do enzymes in the fruit make them soften rapidly once cut, but cut kiwi has also been shown to have greatly reduced vitamin C levels over time.

SWEET POTATOES

A lot of folks think of sweet potatoes as a more orange, sweeter version of the white potato, but sweet potatoes are actually from an entirely different family of plants. And their nutritional benefits are in a whole different world, as well.

QUICK FACTS

1. Sweet potatoes are a great source of beta-carotene, an important antioxidant for eye health.
2. Sweet potatoes contain other antioxidants that have been shown to help improve digestive health.
3. Even though they taste sweet and starchy, sweet potatoes have been shown to actually improve blood sugar regulation, even in people with diabetes.
4. The white potato is not related to the sweet potato.

HEALTH BENEFITS

While sweet potatoes come in numerous hues (orange, yellow, gold, purple), the orange-fleshed version may be one of nature's best sources of the vision-boosting antioxidant beta-carotene.

The antioxidant value of sweet potatoes goes way beyond just beta-carotene, though. Purple sweet potatoes are packed with special antioxidants that may help in particular with issues of the digestive tract.

And while white potatoes have been known to have a negative impact on regulation of blood sugar, sweet potatoes have been proven to actually improve blood sugar regulation—even in people suffering from diabetes.

AVAILABILITY

Although sweet potatoes are often reserved for the Thanksgiving dinner table, many grocery stores will carry them all year-round. Sweet potatoes store well in the proper conditions, so stock up when they are in season and on sale.

HOW TO USE

Sweet potatoes can be used in almost all the same ways white potatoes are used—mashed, roasted, baked, fried. Plus, their sweet flavor also lends itself well to breakfast and dessert.

PORTOBELLO CHEESESTEAKS

This recipe is such a fun (and healthy) twist on the fast-food classic. Portobello mushrooms have a great, meaty texture that works really well in place of the beef that is usually found on cheesesteaks. And by marinating the Portobellos in a smoky vinaigrette, you get a smoky, slow-cooked meat flavor in a vegetarian dish. Perfect for Meatless Mondays!

MAKES: 4 sandwiches
TIME: 45 minutes

For the marinade

2 tablespoons olive oil

1 tablespoon balsamic vinegar

1 clove garlic, minced

1 tablespoon Worcestershire sauce

½ teaspoon salt

½ teaspoon ground black pepper

4 Portobello mushroom caps, stemmed, cut into ½-inch strips

For the sandwiches

2 tablespoons olive oil

1 large bell pepper, seeded and cut into strips

1 large onion, cut into rings

4 slices Swiss cheese

4 whole wheat hoagie buns, sliced in half

To marinate the mushrooms, in a large bowl, whisk together the olive oil, vinegar, garlic, Worcestershire sauce, salt, and pepper. Add the mushroom slices and toss to coat. Let marinate at room temperature for at least 20 minutes.

To prepare the sandwiches, preheat the broiler. Heat the olive oil in a nonstick skillet over medium-high heat. Add the bell pepper and onion, and cook until tender, about 10 minutes. Meanwhile, place the mushrooms (with their marinade mixture) in another nonstick skillet over medium-high heat, and cook until the mushrooms soften and lose most of their moisture, about 10 minutes. Place one-quarter of the mushrooms and one-quarter of the pepper mixture atop the bottom half of each hoagie bun. Place a slice of Swiss on top. Heat under the broiler just until the cheese is melted, about 2 minutes. Remove from the broiler and top with the bun tops.

NUTRITION PER SANDWICH: 431 CALORIES, 24.4 G FAT, 40.5 G CARBS, 16.8 G PROTEIN

GRILLED SALMON PACKETS with Peach Salsa

These superhealthy fish packets use tangy and sweet hard cider as a cooking liquid for the fish. If you don't have any hard cider around, try using orange or apple juice.

MAKES: 2 servings
TIME: 30 minutes

For the salsa

2 medium-size ripe, firm peaches, pitted and diced

1 medium-size red bell pepper, seeded and diced

2 green onions, green and white parts, sliced thinly

¼ cup finely chopped fresh cilantro

1 tablespoon olive oil

1 teaspoon lime juice

1 teaspoon honey

Salt and pepper

For the salmon

1 cup hard cider

1 tablespoon honey

2 dashes Worcestershire sauce

2 (4- to 6-ounce) salmon fillets

Preheat the grill to medium-low heat.

To prepare the salsa, mix together the peaches, bell pepper, green onions, and cilantro. In a separate bowl, whisk together the olive oil, lime juice, honey, and salt and pepper to taste. Drizzle over the peach mixture. Stir and stash in the fridge while preparing remainder of recipe.

To prepare the salmon, in a small saucepan, combine the hard cider, honey, and Worcestershire sauce over medium heat. Bring to a boil, lower the heat, and simmer for 12 to 15 minutes, or until the sauce has reduced by half. Remove from the heat.

To assemble the packets, place each piece of salmon on half of a 12 x 18-inch piece of parchment paper. Drizzle each with half of the cider mixture. Seal up packets by folding the parchment in half and twisting the edge until closed. Place directly on the grill rack. Cook for 10 to 12 minutes. Slice open the packets (watch for steam) and serve with a generous spoonful of the salsa.

NUTRITION PER SERVING: 408 CALORIES, 14.5 G FAT, 33.5 G CARBS, 23.9 G PROTEIN

YOU CAN ALSO
STEAM FRESH
VEGGIES IN THE
PACKET WITH THE
SALMON. I LIKE
ADDING CARROTS,
SNOW PEAS, AND
SWEET PEPPERS.

SALMON

Salmon is the most popular fish on dinner tables in North America, and part of that popularity is due to its incredible nutritional profile. Some folks struggle to get in the recommended two servings per week of seafood, but those recommendations are there for a good reason—fish, especially salmon, is a lean, healthy protein that is packed with nourishing compounds.

QUICK FACTS

1. One of the highest food sources of omega-3s, salmon contains the same amount in one serving that most people get from two to three days' worth of food.
2. This fish is packed with selenium, a nutrient that is important in helping reduce the risk of cardiovascular disease and cancer.

HEALTH BENEFITS

Most of the hype surrounding salmon has focused on its omega-3 content. Salmon is one of the highest sources of omega-3s on the planet, containing the same amount in one serving that most people will get in two to three days' worth of other foods. This high dose of omega-3s is associated with a lowered risk of cardiovascular disease, depression, age-related cognitive disorders, joint inflammation, macular degeneration, and cancer (specifically colorectal, prostate, and breast).

If the powerful benefits of salmon's fatty acids weren't enough to sway you, salmon is also packed with a special protein type that studies have shown to help control inflammation of the digestive tract—in fact, a diet rich in salmon is being lauded by many as an all-natural treatment for ulcerative colitis.

Salmon is also packed with selenium, a nutrient that has been shown to be particularly important in helping prevent cancer and keep cardiovascular disease at bay.

AVAILABILITY

Both fresh and frozen salmon are available in the seafood sections of most supermarkets, but not every salmon package on the shelf is the same. Many salmon varieties carried in stores (both farmed and wild caught) struggle with contamination from pesticides and other pollutants. The lowest risk of contaminated fish comes from varieties labeled "wild Alaskan"—this also happens to be considered the most environmentally friendly source. Other good types of salmon to look for: sockeye, coho, pink, and Chinook.

HOW TO USE

Salmon is a quick-cooking fish that can be broiled, baked, or grilled—it's super versatile. Just make sure you don't overcook your salmon; you're looking for it to be just opaque and flaky, but not dried out. Also, when possible, try to cook the salmon with the skin on, as the highest concentration of omega-3s is located in the flesh that is directly under the skin of the fish, and that flesh is often removed when the skin is removed.

NUTRITION HIGHLIGHTS PER 3 OUNCES SALMON

177	11g	0g	17g	236%	128%	78%
CALORIES	FAT	CARBS	PROTEIN	VITAMIN B12	VITAMIN D	SELENIUM

GINGER

If the closest you get to ginger is a can of your favorite ginger ale, I recommend you try to add this superfood to your diet in more ways than just the fizzy variety. Aside from being a fun and flavorful ingredient to add to cooking, ginger is also packed with health benefits.

QUICK FACTS

1 If you're feeling queasy, ginger is one of the best natural remedies for an upset stomach.

2 As a potent anti-inflammatory, ginger can be a powerful remedy for inflammation-based diseases, such as arthritis.

3 Compounds in ginger makes you sweat, which helps protect you from illness.

4 The flavor and health compounds in ginger are so concentrated, it only takes a little bit to have a big impact.

HEALTH BENEFITS

Ginger's virtues as a pillar in herbal medicine have been touted for millennia. In particular, ginger is widely accepted as one of the best natural methods of alleviating stomach and intestinal upset. In fact, in some studies, ginger has even been shown to be more effective for nausea than some over-the-counter and prescription drugs!

As one of the most potent anti-inflammatories on the planet, ginger is being lauded as a possible treatment for people suffering from arthritis and other inflammation-based ailments.

Studies have also shown than some of the compounds in ginger may help stop the growth of certain cancer cells, and even induce cell death in some cancers. In particular, it looks as though ginger is a powerful agent in helping prevent and fight colorectal and ovarian cancers.

A diet rich in fresh ginger has also been proven to help boost your immune system. Compounds in ginger literally make us sweat more (not just because we're drinking it in hot tea), and that sweat helps protect us from invading infections.

AVAILABILITY

You can find pieces of fresh ginger in the produce section of your local supermarket. Because the health compounds and flavor of ginger are so concentrated, it doesn't take much to make an impact. Thankfully, ginger keeps well in the freezer. Just store it in a resealable plastic freezer bag and lop off pieces as needed.

HOW TO USE

Whenever possible, choose fresh ginger over dried or ground for the most health benefits and best flavor. Ginger stands up well to cooking, and can be used raw or cooked in teas, soups, and many international dishes.

SALMON CAKES

Canned salmon is a great way to get in your weekly dose of fatty fish without breaking your budget. Bonus: Canned salmon is an awesome pantry staple. This recipe makes a great dinner for when you don't know what to make—just head to the pantry, snag a few cans of salmon, and dinner is almost done!

MAKES: 6 servings
TIME: 20 minutes

2 tablespoons butter

1 small red onion, diced

4 stalks celery, diced

1 red bell pepper, seeded and diced

2 (14-ounce) cans salmon, drained

¼ cup minced fresh parsley

2 tablespoons capers

1 teaspoon Worcestershire sauce

1 teaspoon crab boil seasoning
(e.g., Old Bay Seasoning)

1 tablespoon Dijon mustard

2 large eggs

1 cup whole wheat panko bread crumbs

2 tablespoons olive oil

Melt the butter in a medium-size skillet over medium-high heat. Add the onion, celery, and bell pepper and cook until the veggies are tender, about 5 minutes. Remove from the heat. In a large mixing bowl, mash the salmon, using a fork, until no large pieces remain. Add the onion mixture, parsley, capers, Worcestershire sauce, crab boil seasoning, mustard, eggs, and panko. Mix together until well combined. Form into 12 patties. In a large skillet, heat the olive oil over medium-high heat. Add the cakes and cook until browned and crisp, about 5 minutes, then flip and cook for an additional 5 minutes.

NUTRITION PER SERVING: 317 CALORIES, 16.9 G FAT, 13.1 G CARBS, 27.1 G PROTEIN

SERVE THESE WITH FRESH LEMON WEDGES!

SPINACH-RICOTTA STUFFED SHELLS

These stuffed shells are a great dish to serve for Meatless Monday. They're hearty and comforting enough to satisfy the meat eaters in your family, without any meat. As a bonus, they're packed with mega-healthy spinach!

MAKES: *8 servings*
TIME: *1 hour*

12 ounces whole-grain jumbo pasta shells

2 tablespoons olive oil

1 teaspoon dried oregano

1 teaspoon dried basil

1 teaspoon garlic powder

10 ounces frozen spinach, thawed and squeezed dry

16 ounces ricotta cheese

½ cup grated Parmesan cheese

½ cup shredded mozzarella cheese

1 large egg

1 24-ounce jar spaghetti sauce

Preheat the oven to 350°F. Cook the shells according to the package directions, omitting any salt and fat, until just shy of al dente. Drain and set aside. In a medium-size mixing bowl, stir together the olive oil, oregano, basil, garlic powder, spinach, ricotta, Parmesan, mozzarella, and egg. Spoon half of the spaghetti sauce into the bottom of a 9 x 13-inch baking dish. Fill the cooked shells with the ricotta mixture, and place them, open side up, in the baking dish. Pour the remaining sauce over the top of the shells. Bake for 30 to 40 minutes, or until bubbly.

NUTRITION PER SERVING: 333 CALORIES, 11.1 G FAT, 43.7 G CARBS, 16.8 G PROTEIN

THESE SHELLS ARE A
GREAT OPTION FOR
A FREEZER DISH.
FOLLOW THE RECIPE
UNTIL THE STAGE
WHERE YOU PUT
THEM IN THE OVEN,
THEN FREEZE. THAW
THE STUFFED SHELLS
BEFORE BAKING.

SLOW-ROASTED TOMATO SOUP

There are few things more simple and classic than a beautiful bowl of tomato soup. It seems as if even the biggest tomato haters out there can still get behind a nice bowl of tomato soup on a cold, blustery day. This recipe uses slow-roasted canned tomatoes to add tons of flavor.

MAKES: 4 servings
TIME: 1 hour 30 minutes

1 (28-ounce) can whole Italian tomatoes

¼ cup extra-virgin olive oil

1 large bunch basil,
plus several leaves for garnish

Salt and pepper

1 ½ cups milk

THIS RECIPE IS GREAT FOR WINTER BECAUSE IT USES CANNED TOMATOES, WHICH ARE PICKED DURING THEIR PEAK OF FRESHNESS (BOTH TASTE-WISE AND NUTRIENT-WISE) AND THEN CANNED.

Preheat the oven to 300°F. Pour the whole tomatoes into a 9 x 13-inch baking dish. Slice the tomatoes in half. Drizzle with the olive oil. Sprinkle with half of the basil leaves. Season with salt and pepper to taste. Roast the tomatoes for 90 minutes, until the mixture is thickened. Place the tomato mixture in a blender and add the remainder of the basil and the milk. Blend until smooth. Taste and adjust the seasoning. Serve with a drizzle of olive oil and small basil leaves for garnish.

NUTRITION PER SERVING: 207 CALORIES, 14.6 G FAT, 14.5 G CARBS, 5.3 G PROTEIN

DESSERT

~ 206 ~

~ 180 ~

~ 204 ~

~ 192 ~

DARK CHOCOLATE AÇAI BROWNIES
with Date Frosting

Oh man, these brownies are so dark and decadent! Because they're lightly sweetened (and mostly with natural sweeteners, such as applesauce), they are only suitable for the biggest fans of dark chocolate. You might be tempted to skip the frosting on these, but the sugarless date frosting is really what sets these brownies off. It's a fudgy, rich frosting without an ounce of butter, sugar, or cream (and yes, it still tastes amazing).

MAKES: 12 brownies
TIME: 30 minutes (plus chilling time)

For the brownies

⅔ cup unsweetened cocoa powder

½ cup white whole wheat flour

⅓ cup cane sugar

¼ teaspoon baking powder

¼ teaspoon salt

¼ cup coconut oil

⅓ cup unsweetened applesauce

½ cup açai berry puree
(see note about availability on page 10)

1 large egg

1 ½ teaspoons vanilla extract

For the frosting

1 cup pitted Medjool dates
(about 15 whole dates)

½ cup boiling water

⅓ cup unsweetened cocoa powder

½ teaspoon vanilla extract

Pinch of salt

Chopped walnuts for garnish (optional)

To prepare the brownies, preheat the oven to 350°F. Line an 8-inch square baking pan with parchment paper; set aside. In a medium-size mixing bowl, whisk together the cocoa powder, flour, sugar, baking powder, and salt. Add the coconut oil, applesauce, açai berry puree, egg, and vanilla. Stir until just combined; do not overmix. Pour the batter into the prepared pan, spreading it evenly. Bake for 17 to 20 minutes, or until a toothpick inserted into the center comes out clean. Let cool completely before frosting.

To prepare the frosting, place the dates in a blender and pour the boiling water over them. Let the dates soak for about 15 minutes, or until they are very soft. Add the cocoa powder, vanilla, and salt. Pulse the mixture until the frosting is very smooth. Transfer to an airtight container and refrigerate until cold. Once cold, spread on the cooled brownies. Sprinkle with walnuts if using. Slice into 12 brownies.

NUTRITION PER SERVING: 114 CALORIES,
1.5 G FAT, 26.6 G CARBS, 2.8 G CARBS

FEELING GUILTY ABOUT BEING A CHOCOHOLIC? DON'T! LEARN ALL ABOUT HOW DARK CHOCOLATE IS A SUPERFOOD ON PAGE 188.

CHOCOLATE COCONUT ALMOND BUTTER

Homemade almond butter is such a fun (and easy!) thing to make in the kitchen. I love that making it at home gives you complete control. You decide how much sweetener. You decide how much salt. And, in this case, you decide to flavor it with chocolate and coconut. Yum!

MAKES: 1 cup
TIME: 15 minutes

1 cup raw, unsalted almonds

1 cup unsweetened shredded coconut

2 tablespoons unsweetened cocoa powder

1 tablespoon honey

Pinch of salt

In a food processor, combine the almonds and coconut. Process on high speed until the mixture begins to resemble almond butter, about 10 minutes, depending on the strength of your processor. Add the cocoa powder, honey, and salt, and continue to process for an additional 5 minutes, or until the almond butter is smooth and creamy.

NUTRITION PER TABLESPOON:
58 CALORIES, 4.7 G FAT, 3.5 G CARBS, 1.5 G PROTEIN

IF YOU'VE NEVER MADE ALMOND BUTTER AT HOME BEFORE, YOU MIGHT THINK IT'S NEVER GOING TO COME TOGETHER. TRUST ME! EVENTUALLY, THE FRICTION WILL GENERATE ENOUGH HEAT TO MAKE YOUR ALMOND BUTTER SMOOTH AND CREAMY. JUST KEEP AT IT.

BAKED CINNAMON APPLES

Growing up in my house, cinnamon apples were a common weekend supper side dish. It may seem strange to have such a sweet dish on a dinner plate, but they pair beautifully with roasted pork or chicken. The normal cinnamon apple recipe is chock-full of butter and highly processed sugar, but this version keeps it clean with coconut oil and all-natural maple syrup.

MAKES: 4 servings
TIME: 25 minutes

¼ cup coconut oil

¼ cup pure maple syrup

1 teaspoon vanilla extract

2 teaspoons ground cinnamon

⅛ teaspoon ground cloves

⅛ teaspoon ground nutmeg

¼ teaspoon salt

4 tart apples, cored and sliced thinly

Preheat the oven to 375°F. In an oven-safe skillet (I like cast iron) over medium-high heat, melt the coconut oil along with the maple syrup, vanilla, cinnamon, cloves, nutmeg, and salt. Bring the mixture to a boil, lower the heat, and simmer until just slightly thickened. Remove from the heat, add the apple slices, and toss to coat. Place the skillet in the oven for 15 to 20 minutes, stirring every 5 minutes, or until the apple slices are soft and tender and the syrup is thick.

NUTRITION PER SERVING: 207 CALORIES, 13.7 G FAT, 39.5 G CARBS, 0.1 G PROTEIN

IF YOU AREN'T INTERESTED IN SERVING THIS AT SUNDAY DINNER, TRY SERVING WARM WITH A BIG DOLLOP OF VANILLA ICE CREAM FOR DESSERT. YUM!

WHOLE WHEAT BLUEBERRY TARTLETS

These little fruit tartlets are one of the easiest desserts you can make. They whip up in about five minutes, and bake in about 20. The thing that makes these tarts so simple is that the filling is made while the tart is baking in the oven. Whole blueberries go in the oven, and gooey, warm, sweet blueberry jam comes out. It's like magic! Blueberries are naturally high in pectin (the stuff you add to jellies and jams to make them thicken and gel) and when that pectin is heated with just a touch of sugar and flour, you get perfect tart filling.

MAKES: *2 servings*
TIME: *35 minutes*

For the crust

½ cup whole wheat flour

Pinch of salt

1 tablespoon granulated sugar

2 tablespoons cold butter, cut into small pieces

½ teaspoon vanilla extract

Up to 3 teaspoons ice water

For the filling

1 tablespoon granulated sugar

2 teaspoons all-purpose flour

1 cup fresh blueberries

More fresh blueberries and confectioners' sugar for topping

Preheat the oven to 400°F.

To prepare the crust, in a food processor, pulse together the whole wheat flour, salt, and granulated sugar until combined. Add the butter and pulse until the butter pieces are about the size of peas. Add the vanilla and pulse again. Using clean hands, squeeze together a handful of the dough and see whether it sticks together. If it doesn't, pulse in the ice water, 1 teaspoon at a time, until the dough does stick together. Divide the dough between two tart pans and press into shape.

To prepare the filling, in a small bowl, mix together the sugar and flour. Add the cup of blueberries and toss to coat. Divide the blueberry mixture between the two dough-lined tart pans, filling them high (you might have to do some creative stacking). Pour any leftover flour mixture over the two blueberry piles. Place the tart plans on a baking sheet and bake for 20 minutes. Halfway through the baking time, remove the tarts from the oven and give the filling a gentle stir to incorporate any unmelted sugar or flour. Remove the tarts from the oven, let cool for 10 minutes, then press more fresh blueberries into the filling. Sprinkle with confectioners' sugar and serve.

NUTRITION PER SERVING: 307 CALORIES, 13 G FAT, 48 G CARBS, 5 G PROTEIN

CHIA "TAPIOCA" PUDDING

Tapioca pudding is one of my all-time favorite desserts, and one of my favorite things about chia seeds is that they remind me of tapioca! This pudding comes together in a flash, and after a few hours in the fridge, is thick, creamy, and makes for a great dessert or breakfast.

MAKES: 4 servings
TIME: 10 minutes (plus chilling time)

2 cups milk

3 tablespoons honey

1 tablespoon vanilla extract

Pinch of salt

⅓ cup chia seeds

½ teaspoon ground cinnamon

In a medium-size bowl, whisk together the milk, honey, vanilla, and salt. Add the chia seeds and cinnamon and whisk until combined. Cover and refrigerate until thick and creamy, about 3 hours.

NUTRITION PER SERVING: 178 CALORIES, 6.2 G FAT, 25.6 G CARBS, 7.6 G PROTEIN

DRIZZLE THIS PUDDING WITH CHOCOLATE SAUCE FOR A DECADENT DESSERT, OR TOP WITH FRESH BERRIES AND GRANOLA FOR A HEALTHY BREAKFAST.

MAPLE COFFEE ICE CREAM

Coffee ice cream is one of my absolute favorites, and I love making it at home because it gives me control over the caffeine content. I tend to opt for decaf beans so I can eat a bowl of this after dinner without being wired, but if you prefer a little bit of jolt with your dessert, feel free to use caffeinated beans.

MAKES: *about 1 quart*
TIME: *2 hours (plus chilling time)*

2 cups low-fat milk

1 cup half-and-half

¾ cup pure maple syrup

1 ½ cups whole coffee beans

Pinch of salt

5 large egg yolks

½ teaspoon vanilla extract

THIS RECIPE USES LOW-FAT MILK AND HALF-AND-HALF FOR A LIGHTER ICE CREAM; IF YOU WANT A THICKER AND CREAMIER DESSERT, SUB IN WHOLE MILK AND HEAVY CREAM.

In a medium-size saucepan, combine the milk, half-and-half, maple syrup, coffee beans, and salt. Heat over low heat until the mixture just begins to bubble around the edges (do not boil). Continue to cook at this temperature for 10 minutes. Remove from the heat, cover, and let the beans steep in the mixture for an hour, stirring occasionally. When the hour is up, strain the mixture through a sieve and discard the coffee beans. Return the milk mixture to the saucepan, whisk in the egg yolks, and return the pot to the stove over low heat. Heat until bubbles appear around the edges again (do not boil) and the mixture thickens slightly. Remove from the heat, stir in the vanilla, transfer to a heatproof container, and refrigerate until cold, about 2 hours. Spin in ice-cream maker according to the manufacturer's directions. Chill in the freezer until solid.

NUTRITION PER ½-CUP SERVING:
176 CALORIES, 6.9 G FAT, 24.6 G CARBS,
4.7 G PROTEIN

SERVE THIS PUDDING
PARFAIT STYLE, LAYERED
WITH BERRIES, WHIPPED
CREAM, AND CHOPPED
DARK CHOCOLATE,
FOR A SPECIAL TREAT!

DARK CHOCOLATE AVOCADO PUDDING

The thought of avocado as the base for a pudding might turn you off, but I promise this recipe is worth a shot. The avocado is smooth, creamy, and lightly flavored. This just tastes like regular chocolate pudding, but with the added benefit of two powerful superfoods!

MAKES: *4 servings*
TIME: *10 minutes (plus chilling time)*

2 small ripe avocados,
pitted and scooped from skin

⅓ cup plain Greek yogurt

¼ cup skim milk

½ cup unsweetened cocoa powder

½ cup pure maple syrup

1 teaspoon vanilla extract

Pinch of salt

In a food processor, combine the avocados, Greek yogurt, milk, cocoa powder, maple syrup, vanilla, and salt. Process until very smooth. Refrigerate until chilled.

NUTRITION PER SERVING: 357 CALORIES, 21.9 G FAT, 42.5 G CARBS, 6.2 G PROTEIN

DARK CHOCOLATE

Some of the best news to come out of the field of food science in recent years is that chocolate is good for us! Now there is no reason to feel guilty about indulging in a little bit of your favorite chocolaty treat.

QUICK FACTS

1. The darker the better—look for dark chocolate that is at least 85% cacao or more.
2. Chocolate helps lower "bad" cholesterol and keeps the vascular system healthy.
3. It's not all in your head—eating chocolate releases endorphins, which help you feel happy and reduce stress.

HEALTH BENEFITS

It seems that the majority of the benefits of consuming dark chocolate (the darker, the better) are to the cardiovascular system. For a healthy heart, eat more chocolate! The flavonoids and flavanols in chocolate help protect our cells from environmental damage, help keep our vascular system healthy, and may help lower the "bad" cholesterol in our blood.

Raw cacao (which is the building block for dark chocolate) has also been shown to have some of the highest concentrations of several nutrients in our modern diet, including magnesium, which is vital because studies show that some 80 percent of North Americans are deficient in magnesium.

The mental and emotional health benefits of eating chocolate are not to be ignored, either. The act of eating chocolate can release endorphins in our brain that signal us to feel happy and content. These endorphins can help you control your stress levels.

AVAILABILITY

Chocolate is available everywhere, but for the best health benefits, you have to look at the packages with a discerning eye. Very dark chocolate (85 percent cacao or higher) has the most nutrition benefits. The way chocolate is processed can also affect its nutritional impact, so choose organic, fair-trade brands whenever possible. And if you're a big fan of chocolate, you might want to try including raw cacao powder or cacao nibs—it's one of the least processed versions of chocolate available on today's store shelves.

HOW TO USE

Feel free to eat a square of dark chocolate "straight up" as a treat during the day, but also don't forget that chocolate makes an awesome pairing with many other superfoods! Try sprinkling it on your yogurt or in a smoothie.

NUTRITION HIGHLIGHTS PER 1 ½ OUNCES 85% CACAO DARK CHOCOLATE

GOJI BERRY

Also known as wolfberries, goji berries have skyrocketed in popularity in recent years. They are frequently considered one of the most super of the superfoods because of their incredibly high concentration of body-boosting compounds.

QUICK FACTS

❶ One of the most nutritionally dense foods on the planet, goji berries contain 18 amino acids and 21 different vitamins and minerals.

❷ Goji berries are particularly heavy in antioxidants that help protect eye health.

❸ Some research shows that goji berries are powerful in protecting mental health.

HEALTH BENEFITS

The small, red goji berry may look unassuming, but packed inside of that small fruit are 18 amino acids, 21 vitamins and minerals, and a higher concentration of both vitamin C and antioxidants than in almost any other food on the planet. Goji berries are often considered one of the most nutritionally dense foods you can consume!

While goji berries have a wide variety of antioxidants, they are particularly high in carotenoids and zeaxanthin, two compounds that help protect eye health.

Some studies have shown that goji berries are particularly beneficial to mental health. These studies found that goji berry juice, in particular, may help with calmness, alertness, and quality of sleep.

AVAILABILITY

Goji berries grow wild in the Himalayan Mountains, but if you aren't in that region, they can be hard to track down. Luckily, dried goji berries have a very similar nutritional profile and are readily available at most health food stores and some large supermarkets.

HOW TO USE

Dried goji berries can be used like raisins in baking, as snacks, or just for eating by the handful. Some dried goji berries on the market today might be a bit too chewy for you to enjoy, so try soaking the berries in hot water for a few minutes before eating, to rehydrate.

NUTRITION HIGHLIGHTS PER ½ CUP DRIED GOJI BERRIES

177	1g	38g	7.7g	20%	10%	5%
CALORIES	FAT	CARBS	PROTEIN	VITAMIN C	DIETARY FIBER	CALCIUM

GOJI BERRY, COCONUT & DARK CHOCOLATE TRUFFLES

If there is someone out there who you really truly love, you'll make that person a batch of these raw truffles. Why? Well, not only do they taste like the best, richest, most chocolaty truffles you can find at any candy store, but they are also insanely good for you. These naturally sweetened truffles will keep your loved one healthy with the benefits of goji berries, and help keep that person's ticker in tip-top shape, thanks to the dark chocolate. A gift of health is a gift of love!

MAKES: 24 truffles
TIME: 20 minutes

½ cup dried goji berries

1 cup hot water

½ cup coconut oil

1 cup pitted Medjool dates
(about 15 whole dates)

1 tablespoon honey

Pinch of salt

1 teaspoon vanilla extract

1 cup unsweetened, shredded coconut

½ cup unsweetened cocoa powder

Extra coconut or cocoa powder, for garnish

In a small bowl, combine the goji berries and hot water. Let the berries soften for 5 minutes, then drain, squeezing out any excess water. In the basin of a food processor, combine all the ingredients, including the drained goji berries. Pulse until the mixture begins to come together to form a mass. Chill the mixture in refrigerator for 5 minutes to solidify, then, using damp hands, form into 1-inch balls. Roll the balls in extra coconut or cocoa powder, if desired. Store in the fridge.

NUTRITION PER TRUFFLE: 86 CALORIES, 6 G FAT, 9.4 G CARBS, 0.7 G PROTEIN

THESE TRUFFLES CAN BE EASILY VEGANIZED. JUST SWAP OUT THE HONEY FOR AGAVE NECTAR OR PURE MAPLE SYRUP.

BROILED GRAPEFRUIT
with Vanilla Honey

Cooking grapefruit? Who ever heard of such a thing! Don't be afraid. I promise this isn't nearly as strange as it sounds. A quick trip under the broiler brings out the natural sugars of the grapefruit and makes them taste so much more decadent than when you eat them raw. And who says dessert has to be complicated? This one is ready in less than 10 minutes.

MAKES: 4 servings
TIME: 10 minutes

2 red grapefruit, sliced in half

1 vanilla pod

2 tablespoons honey

Pinch of salt

CAN'T FIND VANILLA PODS ANYWHERE? NO PROBLEM. JUST SUB IN A TEASPOON OF HIGH-QUALITY VANILLA EXTRACT.

Preheat the broiler. Using a sharp knife, separate the segments from the membranes of each grapefruit half. Place the grapefruit halves, cut side up, in a shallow baking dish. Using a sharp knife, split the vanilla pod in half lengthwise. Using the knife, scrape the interior of the pod into a small bowl. Add the honey and salt to the bowl, and stir. Drizzle the honey mixture over the grapefruit halves. Place under the broiler and broil for 5 to 7 minutes, or until the tops begin to brown. Serve immediately.

NUTRITION PER SERVING: 52 CALORIES, 0.1 G FAT, 13.8 G CARBS, 0.4 G PROTEIN

RED GRAPEFRUIT & ROSEMARY POPSICLES

As we saw in the Citrus Mint Salad recipe (page 88), grapefruit is an awesome companion for herbs. Here, instead of mint, we're pairing the tart sweetness of grapefruit juice with the smoky flavor of fresh rosemary.

MAKES: 6 popsicles
TIME: 10 minutes (plus freezing time)

1 cup red grapefruit juice
(about 2 large grapefruit)

½ cup coconut water

2 tablespoons honey

1 tablespoon chopped fresh rosemary

Place all the ingredients in a blender. Blend on high speed until well mixed. If the mixture is frothy, let rest for 5 minutes. Then pour into Popsicle mold. Freeze for 3 to 4 hours, or until solid.

NUTRITION PER SERVING: 38 CALORIES, 0.1 G FAT, 9.2 G CARBS, 0.3 G PROTEIN

COCONUT WATER IS A GREAT BASE FOR FRUIT-FLAVORED POPSICLES. IT ADDS A TOUCH OF NATURAL SWEETNESS WITHOUT OVERPOWERING THE FLAVOR OF THE FRUIT.

GREEN TEA PANNA COTTA

A panna cotta sounds like a fancy dessert, but it's actually crazy easy to make! The result is creamy, smooth, and has a hint of green tea flavor that partners really well with a drizzle of honey or a few fresh berries.

MAKES: 4 servings
TIME: 10 minutes (plus chilling time)

1 ½ teaspoons unflavored gelatin

2 tablespoons cold water

1 cup half-and-half

¼ cup honey

1 ½ teaspoons matcha green tea powder

1 cup milk

In a small bowl, combine the gelatin and water; set aside. In a small saucepan, heat the half-and-half and honey over medium-low heat until bubbles begin to show along the edge of the pan (do not boil). Slowly whisk in the matcha powder until dissolved. Remove from the heat, whisk in the gelatin mixture until dissolved, and then add the milk. Pour the mixture into four 6-ounce ramekins. Place the ramekins in the refrigerator and chill until set, about 4 hours.

NUTRITION PER SERVING: 184 CALORIES, 8.2 G FAT, 25.4 G CARBS, 4.6 G PROTEIN

TO UNMOLD, QUICKLY DIP EACH RAMEKIN IN A WARM WATER BATH, AND THEN INVERT ONTO A PLATE.

DARK CHOCOLATE & HEMP SEED FROZEN BANANA BITES

These banana bites are the perfect treat to keep stashed in the freezer for when you need a quick little pick-me-up. Bananas become creamy, frosty and incredibly delicious when they're frozen. These make an awesome healthy treat for kids!

MAKES: 16 bites
TIME: 15 minutes (plus chilling time)

2 large bananas, peeled

6 ounces dark chocolate, chopped

1 tablespoon coconut oil

1 tablespoon hemp seeds

Slice the bananas into ¾- to 1-inch slices; set aside. In a microwave-safe bowl, or in the top part of a double boiler over medium heat, combine the dark chocolate and coconut oil. Heat the mixture in the microwave on high for about a minute, or in the double boiler, until melted and smooth. Dip each banana slice in the melted chocolate mixture and place on a piece of parchment paper. Sprinkle with the hemp seeds. Once all the banana slices are coated, transfer to the freezer and freeze until solid, about an hour. Once they're solid, you can transfer the slices to a resealable plastic freezer bag for storage.

NUTRITION PER BITE: 82 CALORIES, 4.2 G FAT, 10.2 G CARBS, 1.1 G PROTEIN

HEMP SEEDS MAKE A GREAT TOPPER FOR THESE. OTHER AWESOME OPTIONS: CRUSHED PEANUTS, SHREDDED COCONUT, OR EVEN SPRINKLES!

SUPERSEED PEANUT BUTTER CUPS

Healthy peanut butter cups? Yup! Not only do they exist, but you can make them at home in about 15 minutes. For the peanut butter filling, I like to mix in a combo of raw superseeds—not only do they up the nutritional profile of these candies by a ton, but they also add a really satisfying crunch!

MAKES: 12 cups
TIME: 15 minutes (plus chilling time)

6 ounces semisweet chocolate, chopped

1 tablespoon coconut oil

¼ cup natural, unsweetened peanut butter

1 tablespoon honey

1 tablespoon chia seeds

1 tablespoon hemp seeds

1 tablespoon flaxseeds

In a microwave-safe bowl, or in the top part of a double boiler over medium heat, place the dark chocolate and coconut oil. Heat the mixture in the microwave on high for about a minute, or in the double boiler, until melted and smooth. Pour about 1 teaspoon of the chocolate mixture into each of cup of a 12-cup mini muffin tin. Place the tin the freezer to solidify the chocolate, about 3 minutes. Meanwhile, mix together the peanut butter, honey, and seeds in a small bowl. Remove the tin from the freezer, and dollop about 1 teaspoon of the peanut butter mixture on top of the hardened chocolate in each cup, spreading with a spoon to flatten. Top each cup with the remaining chocolate until the peanut butter is covered. Return the tin to the freezer until the chocolate is solid, about 10 minutes. Remove from the tin by placing a knife between the edge of the peanut butter cup and the edge of the tin until the peanut butter cup pops out. Store in an airtight container in the fridge.

NUTRITION PER BITE: 135 CALORIES, 9.3 G FAT, 12.3 G CARBS, 3.2 G PROTEIN

CHIA SEEDS

A decade ago, the only thing you probably knew about chia seeds was that they could grow sprouts that looked like green hair on terra-cotta busts. Now, chia seeds are everywhere! You can find them in snack bars, drinks, and treats throughout the grocery store.

QUICK FACTS

1. Chia is one of the best plant-based sources of omega-3 fatty acids.
2. Chia seeds help keep your body hydrated and lubricated, thanks to their ability to absorb 10 times their weight in water.
3. The gelatinous coating helps slow digestion, resulting in your feeling fuller longer.

HEALTH BENEFITS

Chia seeds are healthy for a number of reasons, but their main claim to fame is that they are one of the highest known plant-based sources of omega-3 fatty acids on the planet. These compounds (the same ones found in fatty fish) are known to help all over the body, including being true brain food—helping to keep your brain synapses firing.

The structure of these little seeds also helps them control cholesterol, weight, and diabetes. When wet, chia seeds have a gelatinous coating that helps slow digestion. Chia seeds are also packed with fiber and protein, both of which help you feel fuller longer.

AVAILABILITY

Chia seeds used to be a specialty item, but now most supermarkets carry the seeds in their health food sections. Chia seeds are also available readily in the bulk sections of most health food stores.

HOW TO USE

The gelatinous nature of chia seeds makes them great for adding to smoothies, yogurt, and hot cereals to add thickness. Use chia seeds just as you would any other nut or seed: sprinkle them on your cup of yogurt, mix them into trail mixes, or use them in granola bars and baked goods.

NUTRITION HIGHLIGHTS PER 2 TABLESPOONS CHIA SEEDS

137	9g	12g	4g	40%	23%	18%
CALORIES	FAT	CARBS	PROTEIN	DIETARY	MAGNESIUM	CALCIUM

HEMP SEEDS

Don't fear the hemp seed! This seed comes from a plant in the marijuana family, but it is a completely legal, 100 percent safe vegetarian protein source that makes a great addition to salads, smoothies, and yogurt. No worries—eating hemp seeds won't get you high; the hemp plant contains only trace amounts (or none at all) of the THC chemical present in marijuana that is considered a drug in many countries.

QUICK FACTS

1 Hemp seeds are a complete vegetarian protein—meaning they contain all the essential amino acids your body needs to get from food sources.

2 The easily digestible protein in hemp is good for people with digestive issues.

3 The balance of omega-3 and omega-6 fatty acids in hemp is perfect for the human body.

HEALTH BENEFITS

Hemp seeds are one of the absolute best and most balanced sources of vegetarian protein. It's one of the few non-animal-based sources of complete protein—meaning it contains all the essential amino acids that aren't produced in our body. The protein in hemp seeds is also easily digestible, making it a great source of protein and healthy fat in those with stomach or colon issues.

These seeds are also one of the few natural sources of both stearidonic acid and gamma-linolenic acid, two omega fatty acids that are easy for the body to process and use.

AVAILABILITY

Check for shelled hemp seeds at your local health food store. You'll also be able to find many hemp products, such as hemp milk, hemp flour, and even hemp ice cream!

HOW TO USE

Hulled hemp seeds make a great mild-flavored, chewy addition to salads, smoothies, and yogurt. Use them in any dish as you would sesame seeds, chia seeds, or flaxseeds, for a boost of complete vegetarian protein.

NUTRITION HIGHLIGHTS PER 3 TABLESPOONS HEMP SEEDS

170	13g	3g	10g	110%	45%	45%
CALORIES	FAT	CARBS	PROTEIN	MANGANESE	MAGNESIUM	PHOSPHORUS

PISTACHIO ICE CREAM with Honey Swirl

This ice cream is a bit different from your typical custard-style ice cream—I think it's a lot easier to make! It uses cornstarch to thicken, and creamy and tangy cream cheese to give it flavor and keep it scoopable even after hours in the freezer.

MAKES: 8 servings
TIME: 40 minutes (plus chilling time)

2 cups low-fat milk, divided

1 tablespoon cornstarch

1 ½ cups half-and-half

½ cup cane sugar

1 cup finely ground, unsalted pistachios

¼ teaspoon salt

½ teaspoon vanilla extract

4 ounces cream cheese, softened

½ cup honey

IT MAY SEEM COUNTERINTUITIVE, BUT MAKE SURE YOU DON'T SWIRL THE HONEY IN WHEN YOU LAYER IT IN THE CONTAINER. IT'LL CREATE A BEAUTIFUL SWIRL WHEN YOU SCOOP IT LATER.

In a small bowl, whisk together 2 tablespoons of the milk with the cornstarch; set aside. In a medium-size saucepan over medium-low heat, heat the remaining milk and the half-and-half and cane sugar until warm and frothy, but not boiling. Remove from the heat and whisk in the pistachios, salt, vanilla, and cream cheese. Continue to whisk until the cream cheese is melted. Return to medium-low heat and whisk in the cornstarch mixture. Continue to cook, stirring constantly, until the mixture is thickened, about 5 minutes. Transfer the mixture to a bowl, and chill in the fridge until completely cold, about 2 hours. Once cold, spin in ice-cream machine according to the manufacturer's instructions. Once done spinning, spoon half of the ice cream into a shallow freezer-safe dish. Drizzle with half of the honey, top with the remaining ice cream, and then the remaining honey. Cover and freeze until hard, about an hour.

NUTRITION PER SERVING: 336 CALORIES, 17.9 G FAT, 40.7 G CARBS, 7.8 G PROTEIN

HONEY

This delicious, golden syrup has been on our breakfast tables for centuries, and even though it's been used anecdotally as medicine since ancient times, the research surrounding health benefits of honey (in particular, local honey) are relatively recent.

QUICK FACTS

1. A powerful antibacterial, antiviral, and anti-inflammatory, honey has been proven better than over-the-counter cough suppressants in studies.
2. Honey is one of the least processed natural sweeteners.
3. Consuming the small amounts of the pollen in local honey may help build your immunity to seasonal allergies.

HEALTH BENEFITS

Honey is one of nature's most natural, least processed, and most nutritious sweeteners. But its benefits go beyond just adding all-natural sweetness to your morning cereal.

You've probably put a bit of honey in your tea when you've felt under the weather, but did you know that adding that honey might actually help you fight your cold? Not only is honey a natural cough suppressant (often performing better in studies than over-the-counter cough suppressants), but it also is a natural antibacterial and antiviral. In fact, it's such a powerful antibacterial that honey is still used today as a salve to treat burns and wounds.

Some studies show that regularly consuming raw, local honey (that includes the pollen of plants in your area) may help you become immune to seasonal allergies. It's not been proven whether this practice is actually helping your body become immune to the pollen, or whether the anti-inflammatory properties of honey are just helping to relieve the congestion and coughing many allergy suffers experience during allergy attacks. Either way, it's a delicious way to feel better!

AVAILABILITY

Honey is sold in supermarkets, but you can find a wide variety of flavors and styles from local bees at your closest health food store or farmers' market. Don't be afraid of honey that is raw, unprocessed, or contains some of the honeycomb!

HOW TO USE

Drizzle a little honey onto anything that needs a touch of sweetness—yogurt, cereal, fruit—anything! You can also skip the processed sweeteners at the coffee bar and instead opt for a spoonful of honey in your morning coffee or tea. Honey also makes an excellent substitute for sugar in baking; just keep in mind that, by volume, honey is sweeter than granulated sugar—use about ⅔ cup of honey for every cup of sugar.

NUTRITION HIGHLIGHTS PER 1 TABLESPOON HONEY

64   0g   17g   0.1g

STRAWBERRY KEFIR POPSICLES

Some folks are turned off by the tangy flavor of kefir, but here the tang works in perfect harmony with the sweetness of honey and strawberries. It's a flavor that'll make anyone a kefir fan!

MAKES: *6 popsicles*
TIME: *5 minutes (plus chilling time)*

1 ½ cups plain kefir

1 cup hulled strawberries

2 tablespoons honey

Combine all the ingredients in a blender and blend on high speed until smooth. Pour into a Popsicle mold and freeze until solid, about 4 hours.

NUTRITION PER POPSICLE: 56 CALORIES, 0.6 G FAT, 10.6 G CARBS, 2.9 G PROTEIN

IF FRESH STRAWBERRIES ARE OUT OF SEASON, YOU CAN SUB IN FROZEN ONES AND GET A TASTY, FROSTY SMOOTHIE!

POMEGRANATE SORBET

This tart and tangy sorbet is less of a dessert and more of a palate cleanser. The low amount of sugar really lets the pomegranate flavor shine through. It's a wonderful way to end a light summer dinner without sending you into a sugar coma.

MAKES: *8 servings*
TIME: *4 hours*

½ cup cane sugar

½ cup water

3 cups chilled, unsweetened pomegranate juice

NOWADAYS, POMEGRANATE JUICE IS READILY AVAILABLE AT MOST SUPERMARKETS; JUST CHECK IN THE REFRIGERATED JUICE SECTION—USUALLY NEAR THE FRESH PRODUCE.

Combine the sugar and water in a small saucepan over medium heat. Stir the mixture until the sugar is completely dissolved. Remove from the heat and stir in the pomegranate juice. Chill the mixture until completely cold—about an hour. Spin in the basin of an ice-cream maker per the manufacturer's instructions. Transfer to a freezer-safe container, and freeze for an additional 2 to 3 hours, or until solid.

NUTRITION PER SERVING: 103 CALORIES, 0 G FAT, 26.8 G CARBS, 0.4 G PROTEIN

DARK CHOCOLATE, POMEGRANATE & PUMPKIN SEED CLUSTERS

These little candies look fancy, but they're incredibly easy to make. Packed up in a pretty box, they make an excellent homemade gift for your favorite health nut.

MAKES: 24 clusters
TIME: 15 minutes

1 ½ cups hulled pumpkin seeds

1 ½ cups pomegranate arils
(about 1 pomegranate's worth)

12 ounces semisweet chocolate, chopped

In a medium-size bowl, toss together the pumpkin seeds and pomegranate arils. Reserve about ¼ cup of the mixture for garnish. In a microwave-safe bowl, or in the top part of a double boiler over medium heat, place the semisweet chocolate. Heat the chocolate in the microwave on high for about a minute, or in the double boiler, until melted and smooth. Pour the chocolate over the seeds, and toss until all the seeds are well coated. Spoon a heaping tablespoon of the mixture onto a piece of parchment paper and then sprinkle with a bit of the reserved seed mixture. Repeat with the remaining chocolate mixture and garnish. Let cool until hardened. Store in an airtight container in the fridge.

NUTRITION PER CLUSTER: 115 CALORIES, 8.2 G FAT, 10.5 G CARBS, 2.7 G PROTEIN

THE BURST OF JUICE FROM THE POMEGRANATE ARILS
IS A REALLY FUN SURPRISE IN THESE CANDIES

PUMPKIN SEEDS

If you've ever roasted the seeds you pull out after carving a pumpkin, you know that these crunchy, nutty seeds are a tasty snack. But don't eat pumpkin seeds just in October! These seeds have so many health benefits, they deserve a spot in your pantry year-round.

QUICK FACTS

1 Pumpkin seeds are a great source of minerals, such as zinc, manganese, phosphorous, copper, and magnesium.

2 A lot of the nutrients in pumpkin seeds are located in a thin skin between the seed and the shell, so eat unhulled seeds.

HEALTH BENEFITS

Because pumpkin plants are low growing and thus have a close proximity to the soil, their seeds are often packed with many of the same minerals you'll find in soil. Pumpkin seeds are one of the best plant-based sources of zinc, manganese, phosphorous, copper, and magnesium available on the market. To get the highest dose of these minerals, eat unhulled pumpkin seeds. The shells don't contain much of the minerals themselves, but there is a thin layer of skin between the seed and the shell that contains high levels—and it's often removed when the seeds are hulled.

AVAILABILITY

You can find hulled and unhulled pumpkin seeds in the bulk bins at many health food stores. You can also roast your own! Just wash and dry the seeds, season with olive oil, salt, and pepper and toast on a baking sheet in a preheated 350°F oven until crisp and brown.

HOW TO USE

Pumpkin seeds make a great snack on their own, but they're also a great addition to granola, salads, and anything that needs a good crunch.

NUTRITION HIGHLIGHTS PER ¼ CUP PUMPKIN SEEDS

224   20g   44g   12g   75%   57%   58%

STRAWBERRIES

There is something about seeing the first pint of these bright red berries at the farmers' market that makes you want to rush home and whip up a strawberry dessert (if you can manage to get them home without eating them all during the trip). But strawberries' benefits go way beyond just being tasty in shortcakes—their nutritional profile makes them a valuable addition to any healthy diet.

QUICK FACTS

1. Strawberries are one of the largest sources of antioxidants in the standard diet.
2. Because the seeds are on the outside of the fruit, strawberries are not considered a true berry.
3. Americans eat an average of 5 pounds of fresh and frozen strawberries per person per year.

HEALTH BENEFITS

Strawberries are a commonplace fruit, but their nutritional value is nothing ordinary. They're consistently ranked among one of the highest sources of powerful antioxidants. And while many fruits and veggies are antioxidant-packed, strawberries are particularly great because of the volume at which people usually consume them. No one just eats one strawberry, and because we tend to chow down on a good-size serving, strawberries are actually one of the most common sources of antioxidants in the standard diet. Those antioxidants help protect the heart, regulate blood sugar, prevent cancer, relieve common digestive ailments (such as Crohn's disease and ulcerative colitis), and reduce incidences of arthritis and eye disease.

AVAILABILITY

Walk into any supermarket at any time of year, and chances are it'll have a big display of strawberries ready for purchase. However, be wary of conventionally grown strawberries. Like most berries, delicate, sweet strawberries require a large amount of pesticides to protect them during growth. Opt for organic berries whenever possible.

Strawberries are a surprisingly fragile fruit, so your best bet is to buy them, at most, a few days before you'll use them. You can also buy and use frozen strawberries with a limited reduction in nutritional value—just make sure to pick up whole frozen berries. Studies show that strawberries that have been sliced or crushed before freezing lose their nutritional value quicker than whole frozen berries do.

HOW TO USE

Raw berries are the best bet for getting the maximum antioxidant benefits, but cooked strawberries also offer a decent amount of nutritional value.

NUTRITION HIGHLIGHTS PER 1 CUP STRAWBERRY HALVES

49	0g	11g	1g	160%	28%	232.6mg
CALORIES	FAT	CARBS	PROTEIN	VITAMIN C	MANGANESE	POTASSIUM

HONEY CORN BREAD STRAWBERRY COBBLER

Fruit cobbler is a summer staple in our house, and we absolutely adore this twist on the standard cakey cobbler. The honey corn bread topping has an incredible texture and flavor that partners beautifully with the strawberry filling. Make sure you serve it up with a big scoop of vanilla ice cream!

THE AMOUNT OF SUGAR YOU NEED TO ADD TO YOUR FILLING DEPENDS ON THE SWEETNESS OF YOUR BERRIES. IF YOU CAN SNAG FRESH BERRIES IN SEASON, YOU MIGHT NOT NEED TO ADD MUCH SUGAR AT ALL.

MAKES: 8 servings
TIME: 1 hour

For the filling

8 cups hulled strawberries

2 tablespoons to ⅓ cup cane sugar

1 tablespoon vanilla extract

1 ½ tablespoons arrowroot powder or cornstarch

For the topping

½ cup cornmeal

½ cup all-purpose flour

½ teaspoon baking soda

Pinch of salt

⅓ cup honey

½ cup low-fat, plain Greek yogurt

1 large egg

¼ cup melted butter

Preheat the oven to 350°F.

To prepare the filling, in a large bowl, stir together the strawberries, sugar, vanilla, and arrowroot powder until the strawberries are coated in the mixture. Pour the strawberry mixture into a 9 x 13-inch baking dish; set aside.

To prepare the topping, in a medium-size mixing bowl, whisk together the cornmeal, flour, baking soda, and salt. In a small-size mixing bowl, whisk together the honey, Greek yogurt, egg, and melted butter. Pour the liquid ingredients into the dry ingredients and stir to combine—do not overmix. Spoon the batter on top of the strawberries in large dollops—no need to spread it. Bake for 40 to 50 minutes, or until the corn bread topping is golden brown and the filling is thick and bubbly. If the topping begins to brown before the filling is finished, tent it with aluminum foil to prevent burning.

NUTRITION PER SERVING: 247 CALORIES, 7.1 G FAT, 43.2 G CARBS, 4.7 G PROTEIN

WATERMELON GRANITA

Making a granita is a simple solution when the weather is toasty and you're craving a homemade icy treat. Granitas use only two ingredients—fruit and sweetener—and results in the best snow cone you've ever had!

MAKES: 4 servings
TIME: 4 hours

4 cups cubed seedless watermelon

Zest and juice of 1 lime

2 tablespoons honey

THIS FROZEN DESSERT REQUIRES NO SPECIAL EQUIPMENT TO MAKE— PERFECT FOR WHEN THE THERMOMETER IS MAXED OUT AND YOU'RE TOO CRANKY TO DIG AROUND IN THE PANTRY FOR AN ICE-CREAM MAKER.

In a blender, combine all the ingredients. Pulse until smooth. Pour the mixture into an 9 x 13-inch baking dish, cover with plastic wrap, and place flat in freezer. After an hour in the freezer, scrape the frozen portion of the mixture using a fork to create slushy ice. Place back in the freezer and repeat the process every hour until the entire mixture is frozen and slushy, about 3 hours.

NUTRITION PER SERVING: 67 CALORIES, 0 G FAT, 18.1 G CARBS, 0.5 G PROTEIN

WATERMELON

Summertime means watermelon! These perfectly sweet melons are staples at summer barbecues. And as a bonus, they are one of the healthiest and most nutrient-dense fruits on the market.

QUICK FACTS

❶ Watermelon is loaded with the heart-healthy antioxidant lycopene.
❷ Watermelon is a decent source of immune-boosting vitamin C.
❸ Due to its high water content, watermelon is a very hydrating food.

HEALTH BENEFITS

Just like their red-colored friends tomatoes, watermelons are packed with lycopene, an important antioxidant for bone health and cardiovascular health.

Watermelon is also an excellent source of vitamin C in relation to its calorie content. For less than 50 calories of watermelon, you get 16 percent of your vitamin C recommended daily allowance.

One promising aspect of watermelon is its citrulline content, an amino acid that that supports cardiovascular and muscular health.

AVAILABILITY

While watermelon is available in most supermarkets year-round, to get the highest nutrient content, look for watermelon that is vine-ripened during the summer. The nutritional difference between watermelon harvested and shipped during winter months versus fresh, local watermelon is drastic.

HOW TO USE

Watermelon doesn't hold up well to cooking, so the best way to use it is raw. Cut it up and eat it fresh, or use it in smoothies, other drinks, and warm-weather desserts.

NUTRITION HIGHLIGHTS PER 1 CUP WATERMELON CUBES

46	0.2g	11g	0.9g	16%	7%	5%
CALORIES	FAT	CARBS	PROTEIN	VITAMIN C	COPPER	POTASSIUM

YOGURT

One of the quintessential health foods, yogurt has been stocked in the fridges of healthy eaters for decades. The tangy flavor of yogurt lends itself well to cooking and baking, and it mixes beautifully with fresh fruit, nuts, seeds, and other superfoods for a meal or a snack.

QUICK FACTS

❶ Yogurt is loaded with healthy living bacteria that help balance the digestive system.

❷ Yogurt is a great source of calcium and vitamin D, important for bone health.

HEALTH BENEFITS

Yogurt is packed with probiotics—healthy bacteria that help balance your digestive tract. These healthy bacteria have also been shown to help balance blood sugar. These living bacteria also provide us with a wide variety of nutrients and minerals.

As are most dairy foods, yogurt is also an excellent source of calcium and vitamin D—important nutrients in maintaining bone health.

AVAILABILITY

The yogurt section of your local supermarket is probably big, overwhelming, and full of brightly colored packaging. Unfortunately, most of the yogurts in the dairy case are loaded with artificial flavors, artificial colors, and sugar. For the best health benefits, stick with plain yogurt, and, if possible, yogurt made organically. Studies have shown that milk from grass-fed cows makes the most nutrient-dense yogurt.

If you prefer flavored yogurt, try flavoring your own by mixing honey, berries, or nuts and seeds into plain yogurt.

HOW TO USE

We've all eaten yogurt as a snack or as a part of a balanced breakfast, but yogurt's uses go way beyond the spoon. Yogurt can be used in place of many dairy products in cooking and baking.

NUTRITION HIGHLIGHTS PER 1 CUP PLAIN, WHOLE-MILK YOGURT

LEMON YOGURT CAKE

This cake is a dessert that I like to use to fool the masses. It's so flavorful, so moist, and so incredibly delicious that you could serve it to even the pickiest haters of health food and they'd swoon over your decadent dessert–making skills— without ever knowing it's 100 percent whole wheat, sweetened with natural sugars, and packed with gut-healthy yogurt.

MAKES: *16 servings*
TIME: *1 hour (plus cooling time)*

For the cake

Cooking spray

3 cups white whole wheat flour

1 tablespoon baking powder

½ teaspoon salt

1 cup cane sugar

2 cups plain, low-fat yogurt

3 large eggs

Zest and juice of 2 large lemons

1 teaspoon vanilla extract

½ cup coconut oil, melted

½ cup unsweetened applesauce

For the glaze

1 cup confectioners' sugar

2 tablespoons lemon juice

To prepare the cake, preheat the oven to 350°F. Spray a small Bundt pan liberally with cooking spray; set aside. In a large bowl, sift together the flour, baking powder, salt, and sugar. In a medium-size bowl, whisk together the yogurt, eggs, lemon zest and juice, vanilla, coconut oil, and applesauce until smooth. Pour into the flour mixture and stir until well combined. The batter will be thick. Spoon the batter into the prepared pan and smooth out the surface. Bake for 45 to 50 minutes, or until a toothpick inserted into the center of the cake comes out clean. Remove from the oven and let cool completely in the pan.

To prepare the glaze, whisk together the confectioners' sugar and lemon juice. Invert the cake onto a plate, and pour the glaze over top.

NUTRITION PER SERVING: 259 CALORIES, 8.3 G FAT, 41.5 G CARBS, 5.2 G PROTEIN

IF YOU AREN'T A FAN OF THE HIGHLY PROCESSED CONFECTIONERS'
SUGAR IN THE GLAZE, SKIP IT! THE CAKE IS WONDERFULLY MOIST
AND FLAVORFUL WITHOUT ANY GLAZE OR FROSTING.

5

SNACKS & SIDES

≈ 254 ≈   ≈ 264 ≈   ≈ 232 ≈   ≈ 228 ≈

AÇAI-CHIA JAM & GOAT CHEESE CROSTINI

Crostini **may sound like something fancy and fussy, but it really just means "little toasts" in Italian. And even though you can make these tasty appetizers in about 15 minutes, it doesn't mean they aren't impressive enough to serve to guests at your next dinner party. People will ooh and aah when you serve them!**

MAKES: *20 slices*
TIME: *15 minutes*

For the jam

½ cup açai berry puree
(see note about availability on page 10)

3 tablespoons chia seeds

3 tablespoons cane sugar

2 tablespoons balsamic vinegar

For the crostini

1 multigrain baguette, cut into 1-inch slices

¼ cup olive oil

Salt and pepper

6 ounces soft goat cheese

Fresh chives or sage leaves, for garnish

Preheat the oven to 400°F. To prepare the jam, in a small saucepan, combine all the jam ingredients. Bring to a boil, lower the heat, and simmer until the jam is thick, about 5 minutes. Remove from the heat, transfer to a heatproof bowl, and store in the fridge while you prepare the crostini.

To prepare the crostini, using a pastry brush, brush the olive oil onto both sides of each slice of the bread. Place on a baking sheet. Sprinkle each slice with salt and pepper to taste. Toast in the oven for 5 to 7 minutes, or until golden brown and crispy. Remove from the oven, and spread about a tablespoon of goat cheese and a tablespoon of jam onto each toast slice. Top with chives or sage leaves. Serve immediately.

NUTRITION PER SLICE: 136 CALORIES, 5.7 G FAT, 17 G CARBS, 5.1 G PROTEIN

YOU CAN PREP ALL THE ELEMENTS FOR THIS AHEAD OF TIME (INCLUDING THE TOASTS— JUST STORE THEM IN AN AIRTIGHT CONTAINER AT ROOM TEMPERATURE), AND JUST ASSEMBLE THE TOASTS WHEN IT'S TIME TO SERVE.

SWEET & SPICY ALMONDS

Oh man, these almonds are incredibly addicting. So addicting, they seem to magically disappear whenever I make them! Add these to your spread the next time you host game night. Your guests will be begging for the recipe.

MAKES: 2 cups
TIME: 15 minutes

2 cups raw, unsalted almonds

1 tablespoon honey

1 tablespoon water

1 teaspoon olive oil

¼ cup cane sugar

2 teaspoons salt

¾ teaspoon cayenne pepper

THIS RECIPE MAKES A MEDIUM-SPICY ALMOND, WHICH IS GOOD FOR A MIXED GROUP OF PEOPLE. IF YOU'RE REALLY INTO HEAT, KICK UP THE CAYENNE PEPPER TO A FULL TEASPOON OR MORE.

Preheat the oven to 350°F. Spread out the almonds in a single layer on an ungreased baking sheet. Toast in the oven until the almonds are fragrant and just beginning to brown, about 10 minutes. Meanwhile, whisk together the honey, water, and olive oil in a small bowl. In another small bowl, mix together the sugar, salt, and cayenne. When the almonds have finished toasting, drizzle with the honey mixture, and toss until each almond is coated. Sprinkle with the sugar mixture, and toss to coat. Spread out the almonds on a piece of parchment paper to cool and harden.

NUTRITION PER ¼ CUP: 174 CALORIES, 12.5 G FAT, 13.6 G CARBS, 5.0 G PROTEIN

SESAME & AMARANTH CRACKERS

These gluten-free crackers are incredibly simple to make, and they're so much more flavorful than anything you can buy on store shelves! Serve 'em up as a crunchy side to a salad or as a dipper for hummus.

MAKES: *about 80 crackers*
TIME: *about 30 minutes*

2 cups amaranth flour

1 cup sesame seeds

3 tablespoons olive oil

3 large eggs

1 teaspoon salt

1 tablespoon water

MOST SUPERMARKETS NOW CARRY AMARANTH FLOUR IN THEIR GLUTEN-FREE OR HEALTH FOOD SECTIONS, BUT IF YOU'RE HAVING A HARD TIME TRACKING IT DOWN, JUST GRIND UP WHOLE AMARANTH SEEDS IN A COFFEE GRINDER.

Preheat the oven to 350°F. In a bowl, combine the amaranth flour, sesame seeds, olive oil, eggs, salt, and water until the mixture forms a crumbly dough that holds together when squeezed. Form the dough into two disks. Lay a piece of parchment paper on a flat surface, place one of the disks on top, and cover with another piece of parchment. Roll the dough into a rectangle about ⅛ inch thick. Remove the top piece of parchment, and using a pizza cutter or sharp knife, cut into 1-inch squares. Transfer the crackers (including the lower parchment paper) to a baking sheet and bake for 15 to 20 minutes, or until the crackers are browned and crisp. Repeat with the remaining dough disk.

NUTRITION PER 5 CRACKERS: 177 CALORIES, 9.6 G FAT, 18.3 G CARBS, 6.2 G PROTEIN

CREAMY AVOCADO VINAIGRETTE

This healthy salad dressing comes together in about five minutes. The compounds in avocados help your body absorb antioxidants, so if you want to make sure you're getting the most out of your salad— use this dressing!

MAKES: *12 servings*
TIME: *5 minutes*

1 ripe avocado, pitted and scooped from skin

⅓ cup white wine vinegar

Juice of 1 lemon

Salt and pepper

¾ cup extra-virgin olive oil

In a food processor, combine the avocado, vinegar, lemon juice, and salt and pepper to taste. Process until very smooth and creamy. With the processor running on low speed, stream in the olive oil through the chute until just combined.

NUTRITION PER SERVING: 144 CALORIES, 15.9 G FAT, 1.5 G CARBS, 0.3 G PROTEIN

THIS VINAIGRETTE
STORES NICELY
IN AN AIRTIGHT
CONTAINER IN
THE FRIDGE.

CHOCOLATE-COFFEE ENERGY BITES

No need for energy drinks or shots—these supertasty bites are made with all-natural ingredients, including a touch of ground coffee to give you a small burst of caffeine when you need it most. Each bite contains about 35 mg of caffeine (depending on the coffee you use)—which is equal to about half a cup of brewed coffee.

MAKES: *12 bites*
TIME: *5 minutes*

1 cup pitted Medjool dates
(about 15 whole dates)

½ cup raw almonds

¼ cup unsweetened cocoa powder

2 tablespoons ground coffee

1 tablespoon chia seeds

Pinch of salt

Combine all the ingredients in a food processor. Pulse until the almonds are in very small pieces and the mixture holds together when squeezed. Using wet hands, form into twelve 1-inch balls.

NUTRITION PER SERVING: 50 CALORIES, 3.0 G FAT, 6.1 G CARBS, 1.8 G PROTEIN

WANT THE FLAVOR WITHOUT THE BUZZ? JUST SUB IN DECAF COFFEE.

ORANGE BALSAMIC GLAZED BEETS

I used to be a beet hater, but this recipe was the one that started me on a path to beet loving! The sweet and tangy glaze helps balance out the earthiness of the beets that a lot of folks don't like.

MAKES: 4 servings
TIME: 1 hour 30 minutes

For the beets

6 large beets, scrubbed and greens removed

2 tablespoons olive oil

Salt and pepper

For the glaze

Juice and zest of 2 oranges

½ cup balsamic vinegar

2 tablespoons honey

THIS RECIPE WORKS WITH BOTH PURPLE AND GOLDEN BEETS—FOR A PRETTY PLATTER, MIX THE TWO!

To prepare the beets, preheat the oven to 400°F. Rub the beets with the olive oil and sprinkle with salt and pepper. Wrap each of the beets tightly in aluminum foil. Place in a small baking dish and bake for 40 to 50 minutes, or until fork tender. Let cool until the beets can be handled.

While the beets cool, prepare the glaze. In a small saucepan, mix the orange juice and zest, vinegar, and honey. Bring to a boil, lower the heat to a simmer, and cook for 10 to 15 minutes, or until the glaze becomes thick and syrupy.

Once the beets are cool, peel off outer skins and then chop the beets into bite-size pieces. Toss the beets with the glaze and season with additional salt and pepper, if needed.

NUTRITION PER SERVING: 186 CALORIES, 7.3 G FAT, 29.3 G CARBS, 3.0 G PROTEIN

BAKED SWEET POTATO FRIES
with Garlic-Avocado Aioli

If you've ever tried to make sweet potato fries at home and ended up with less-than-crispy results, I've got the solution for you—cornstarch! Sweet potatoes release a lot of moisture when baking, and tossing them ahead of time in cornstarch helps absorb the moisture and crisp up.

MAKES: 4 servings
TIME: 30 minutes

For the fries

3 tablespoons cornstarch

1 tablespoon paprika

1 teaspoon garlic powder

1 teaspoon salt

½ teaspoon ground cinnamon

Pinch of cayenne pepper

2 large sweet potatoes, peeled and cut into fries

2 tablespoons olive oil

For the aioli

1 large, ripe avocado, pitted and scooped from skin

½ cup mayonnaise

3 cloves garlic

Juice of ½ lemon

Salt and pepper

To prepare the fries, preheat the oven to 400°F. Line two large baking sheets with parchment paper; set aside. In a small bowl, whisk together the cornstarch, paprika, garlic powder, salt, cinnamon, and cayenne. Toss the sweet potatoes with the olive oil, and then toss with the cornstarch mixture. Spread out the fries in a single layer on the prepared baking sheets, being careful not to crowd them (this causes them to steam instead of baking, making for mushy fries). Bake for 25 to 30 minutes, or until the fries are browned and crisp.

While the fries are baking, prepare the aioli by mixing together all the aioli ingredients in a food processor. Pulse until very smooth. Serve with the warm fries.

NUTRITION PER SERVING:
311 CALORIES, 26.9 G FAT,
19.3 G CARBS, 1.8 G PROTEIN

THIS AIOLI ISN'T JUST FOR DIPPING FRIES. TRY IT ON TOP OF BURGERS, AS A FUN ADDITION TO GRILLED CHEESE, OR IN PLACE OF MAYO ON SANDWICHES.

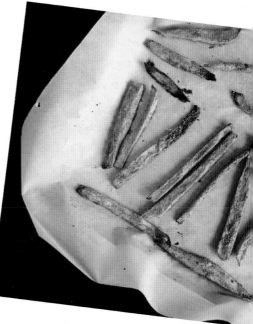

LEMON-GARLIC WHITE BEAN HUMMUS

Hummus is traditionally made with chickpeas, and while the result is fine, I prefer using white beans as the base for my hummus because they result in the smoothest and creamiest dip! Plus, you still get the same fiber and protein benefits as you would if you used chickpeas.

MAKES: 8 servings
TIME: 10 minutes

2 (14-ounce) cans Great Northern beans, drained and rinsed

Juice of 2 lemons

¼ cup tahini

4 cloves garlic, peeled

½ teaspoon salt

¼ teaspoon hot sauce

¼ cup extra-virgin olive oil

In a food processor, mix together the beans, lemon juice, tahini, garlic, salt, and hot sauce. Process until the beans are smooth, stopping to scrape the sides if necessary. With the processor running on low speed, stream in the olive oil through the chute and process until just combined.

NUTRITION PER SERVING: 194 CALORIES, 11.2 G FAT, 22.0 G CARBS, 6.3 G PROTEIN

IF YOU'RE A HUGE GARLIC FAN, FEEL FREE TO TOSS IN A FEW MORE CLOVES FOR AN EXTRA KICK (AND MAYBE KEEP THE BREATH MINTS NEARBY).

ROASTED GARLIC WHOLE WHEAT FOCACCIA

Focaccia is one of the easiest of the yeast breads to make at home—it's really hard to mess up! This version is flavored with garlic-infused olive oil and slow-roasted garlic cloves. It makes an awesome side for pasta dishes, or cut into large pieces and use it as bread for your favorite sandwich.

MAKES: *8 servings*
TIME: *1 hour 30 minutes*

Cooking spray

½ cup plus 2 tablespoons olive oil, divided

1 head garlic, halved lengthwise

2 ½ teaspoons active dry yeast

3 ¼ cups white whole wheat flour

1 teaspoon salt

1 ⅔ cups warm water

1 tablespoon honey

1 tablespoon Italian seasoning

THIS BREAD STASHES WELL IN THE FREEZER. JUST POP IT IN THE OVEN FOR 10 MINUTES OUT OF THE FREEZER TO WARM BEFORE SERVING.

Preheat the oven to 300°F. Spray a 9 x 13-inch baking dish with cooking spray; set aside. Pour ½ cup of the olive oil in a small baking dish and place the garlic, cut side down, in the olive oil. Bake for 25 to 30 minutes, or until the cloves are tender. Remove the garlic from the oil, reserving the oil, and remove the cloves from their paper wrappers. Set aside. Increase the oven temperature to 375°F. Meanwhile, in the bowl of a stand mixer fitted with a dough hook, combine the yeast, flour, and salt. Add the 2 remaining tablespoons of olive oil, the water, and the honey, and mix on low speed until the dough comes together. The dough will be wet and sticky. Spread out the dough in the prepared baking dish, using greased hands to press it evenly to the edge. Cover with plastic wrap and let rise until puffy, about 30 minutes.

After the rising time, using the handle of a wooden spoon, push multiple holes in the surface of the bread. Drizzle with the garlic-infused olive oil, push the roasted garlic cloves into the surface of the bread, and sprinkle with the Italian seasoning. Cover again with plastic wrap and let rise for an additional 15 minutes. Bake for 15 to 20 minutes, or until the top of the bread just begins to brown. Let cool for 10 minutes before cutting into 16 slices.

NUTRITION PER SERVING: 289 CALORIES, 14.0 G FAT, 37.3 G CARBS, 7.1 G PROTEIN

GREEN TEA LEMONADE

Normally, when we think about drinking green tea, we envision sipping on a steaming mug of the good stuff by a cozy fireplace with a good book. But green tea doesn't have to be just for the cold-weather months! This crisp and cool lemonade is a great way to get your green tea fill in warmer weather.

MAKES: 4 servings
TIME: 10 minutes

½ cup cane sugar

3 green tea bags

1 ½ cups boiling water

Juice of 3 lemons (about ½ cup)

1 cup cold water

Ice cubes

Place the sugar and tea bags in a heatproof pitcher. Pour in the boiling water, and stir to dissolve the sugar. Let the tea bags steep for 3 minutes. Remove the tea bags. Add the lemon juice, water, and ice cubes. Stir until the lemonade is cold. Add more ice cubes if necessary.

NUTRITION PER SERVING:
101 CALORIES, 0.2 G FAT,
25.6 G CARBS, 0.2 G PROTEIN

IF YOU'RE SERVING IN A CLEAR CONTAINER, ADDING SOME THINLY SLICED LEMON MAKES FOR A BEAUTIFUL APPEARANCE.

HONEY-GLAZED CARROTS

These sweet and savory carrots make an awesome superfood side for your favorite dinner. This glazing method also works well with sweet potatoes.

MAKES: *4 servings*
TIME: *20 minutes*

2 tablespoons coconut oil

6 large carrots, peeled and cut into ½-inch pieces

1 teaspoon salt

1 cup chicken or vegetable broth

3 tablespoons honey

Juice of ½ lemon

Ground black pepper

Melt the coconut oil over medium-high heat in a large skillet, add the carrots and salt, and sauté until the carrots begin to brown and soften. Add the broth and honey, bring to a boil, lower the heat, and simmer until the carrots are tender and the liquid is thick and syrupy. Remove from the heat, squeeze on the lemon juice, and season with ground pepper to taste.

NUTRITION PER SERVING: 160 CALORIES, 7.4 G FAT, 23.6 G CARBS, 2.3 G PROTEIN

IF YOU AREN'T A FAN OF THE COCONUT FLAVOR FROM THE COCONUT OIL, YOU CAN SUB IN BUTTER.

HONEY FLAX BREAD

I used to be petrified of baking my own bread. There is something about the chemistry of the yeast that always scared me away! But once I took the plunge, I was hooked. There is nothing tastier (or better smelling) than freshly baked bread. This simple wholegrain bread recipe is a good place to start if you're intimidated.

MAKES: *12 slices*
TIME: *3 hours*

1 cup warm water

2 tablespoons olive oil

¼ cup honey

2 ½ teaspoons active dry yeast

3 ⅔ cups white whole wheat flour

1 cup ground flaxseeds

⅔ cup milk

1 ½ teaspoons salt

1 tablespoon whole flaxseeds

In the bowl of a stand mixer fitted with the dough hook, stir together the water, olive oil, and honey. Sprinkle with the yeast and let rest until white and frothy, about 5 minutes. Add the flour, ground flaxseeds, milk, and salt. With the mixer on low speed, knead the mixture for about 15 minutes, or until the dough is stretchy and smooth (but still a bit sticky). Transfer the dough to a clean, greased bowl and cover with plastic wrap. Let rise in a warm area until doubled in size, about 90 minutes. Preheat the oven to 350°F. After the rising time, form the dough into a loaf shape and transfer to a greased loaf pan. Sprinkle the whole flaxseeds on top, cover loosely with plastic wrap, and let rise again until the dough crests the edge of the pan by an inch, about 45 minutes. Remove the plastic wrap and bake the loaf for 35 to 40 minutes, or until the bread is browned and crusty. Let cool completely before slicing.

NUTRITION PER SLICE: 241 CALORIES, 7.9 G FAT, 33.1 G CARBS, 9.7 G PROTEIN

TOP A WARM SLICE OF THIS BREAD WITH ROASTED PISTACHIO & PUMPKIN SEED BUTTER (PAGE 253) FOR A DOUBLE DOSE OF SUPERSEEDS!

SALSA VERDE WITH KIWI

This green salsa is made using tart and tangy tomatillos—which are available nowadays in the produce section of most supermarkets. The kiwis add a delicious sweetness that is really delicious atop savory dishes.

MAKES: 4 servings
TIME: 20 minutes

6 tomatillos, husks removed

2 kiwis, peeled

1 small onion, roughly chopped

½ cup fresh cilantro leaves

Juice of 1 lime

1 jalapeño, seeds and membranes removed

Salt

Preheat the broiler. Place the tomatillos in a small baking dish, and roast under the broiler until soft and browned, about 15 minutes. Pour the roasted tomatillos and their juice into a blender, add all remaining ingredients, including salt to taste, and blend until smooth. Chill in the refrigerator until cold.

NUTRITION PER SERVING: 49 CALORIES, 0.8 G FAT, 10.5 G CARBS, 1.1 G PROTEIN

YOU CAN'T BEAT THIS SALSA ON TOP OF FISH OR SHRIMP TACOS!

PARMESAN & SAUSAGE-STUFFED MUSHROOMS

This appetizer is a favorite in my family. When these little bubbly mushroom caps come out of the oven at any of our family events, they're lucky if they can make it to a serving dish before they're gone. They're so good, and so incredibly easy to whip up!

MAKES: *3 dozen*
TIME: *50 minutes*

Cooking spray

24 ounces large button mushrooms (about 36 mushrooms total)

1 pound mild Italian sausage

2 cloves garlic, minced

1 tablespoon fresh minced sage

½ cup shredded Parmesan cheese

Preheat the oven to 350°F. Spray a baking sheet with cooking spray and set aside. Wash the mushrooms and remove the stems, setting the mushroom caps aside. Dice the mushroom stems finely and then combine with the sausage, garlic, sage, and Parmesan. The best way to mix the combo is with clean hands. Overfill each mushroom cap with the sausage mixture—mounding a pile on top. Place on the prepared baking sheet. When all the caps are filled, bake for 35 to 40 minutes, or until the sausage is cooked through.

NUTRITION PER MUSHROOM:
53 CALORIES, 4 G FAT, 1 G CARBS,
3 G PROTEIN

IF YOU HAVE ANY LEFTOVER FILLING, ROLL IT INTO MEATBALLS, SAUTÉ, AND SERVE WITH SPAGHETTI. YUM!

ROASTED PISTACHIO & PUMPKIN SEED BUTTER

If you've never made your own nut butter before, it might seem like a complicated process, but it's actually incredibly easy if you have a food processor and a little bit of patience. This combination is a great place to start; it gives you a thick, creamy, richly flavored nut butter that is great on toast.

MAKES: 1 cup
TIME: 15 minutes

1 ½ cups salted pistachio meats

1 cup raw, unhulled pumpkin seeds

1 teaspoon vanilla extract

1 tablespoon honey

Preheat the oven to 350°F. Spread out the pistachios and pumpkin seeds in a single layer on an ungreased baking sheet. Toast for about 5 minutes, or until they become fragrant. Remove from the oven and place in a food processor. Process until the mixture becomes a paste, about 10 minutes. Add the vanilla and honey, and process until smooth and creamy.

NUTRITION PER TABLESPOON:
118 CALORIES, 9.3 G FAT, 6.0 G CARBS,
4.6 G PROTEIN

IF YOU USE UNSALTED PISTACHIOS, ADD A PINCH OR TWO OF SALT WHILE PROCESSING.

STRAWBERRY LIMEADE

If you could put summer in a glass, it would taste exactly like this limeade. This lightly sweet, tangy fruit drink is perfect for the whole family (and works really well as a base for an adult beverage with white rum or vodka added). It's pretty hard to beat a tall, cold glass of strawberry limeade to end a hot summer day!

MAKES: 6 servings
TIME: 10 minutes

4 cups water

⅔ cup cane sugar

2 cups ice cubes, plus more for glasses

1 ½ cups sliced, hulled strawberries

½ cup lime juice

Lime slices, for garnish

In a medium-size saucepan, combine the water and sugar over medium-high heat. Stir until the sugar is dissolved, about 5 minutes. Remove from the heat, and stir in the 2 cups of ice cubes until melted. Place the sugar syrup, strawberries, and lime juice in a blender and blend until combined. Pour over ice in glasses, and garnish with lime slices.

NUTRITION PER SERVING: 99 CALORIES, 0.2 G FAT, 26.4 G CARBS, 0.3 G PROTEIN

THIS LIMEADE IS GREAT BY ITSELF, BUT IT ALSO MAKES A FUN TWIST ON AN ARNOLD PALMER (JUST SPLIT ONE PART LIMEADE TO ONE PART SWEETENED ICED TEA) OR A SHANDY (ONE PART LIMEADE TO ONE PART BEER).

QUINOA WITH SWEET POTATOES & CRANBERRIES

This vegetarian dish is a great, fall-flavored option for your Thanksgiving dinner table. And best of all, the leftovers just get better and better as they meld in the fridge! This is a Thanksgiving leftover you'll love to eat for days after turkey day.

MAKES: *6 servings*
TIME: *45 minutes*

For the quinoa

2 cups chicken or vegetable broth

1 cup quinoa

2 large sweet potatoes, peeled and chopped into bite-size pieces

2 large apples, cored and chopped into bite-size pieces

1 large onion, chopped into bite-size pieces

2 cloves garlic, minced

½ teaspoon ground cinnamon

½ teaspoon salt

¼ teaspoon ground black pepper

¼ teaspoon olive oil

½ cup dried cranberries

½ cup toasted chopped walnuts

For the dressing

2 tablespoons olive oil

1 tablespoon cider vinegar

1 tablespoon lemon juice

1 tablespoon pure maple syrup

1 tablespoon spicy brown mustard

Salt and pepper

To prepare the beets, Preheat the oven to 375°F. Line a baking sheet with parchment paper. Set aside.

In a saucepan, bring the broth to a boil over medium-high heat. Add the quinoa, lower the heat and simmer until quinoa is tender and has absorbed all the liquid, about 10 minutes. Set aside.

Toss together the sweet potatoes, apples, onion, and garlic. In a small bowl, whisk together the cinnamon, salt, pepper, and olive oil. Pour over sweet potato mixture and toss to coat. Spread out the mixture in one layer on the prepared baking sheet. Roast for 15 to 20 minutes, or until all the veggies are tender.

To prepare the dressing, whisk together all the ingredients until well combined, adding salt and pepper to taste.

To assemble the salad, toss together the quinoa, roasted veggies, cranberries, walnuts, and dressing until well combined. Serve immediately, or refrigerate and serve cold, or heat and serve warm for a more intense flavor.

NUTRITION PER SERVING: 340 CALORIES, 13.2 G FAT, 48.8 G CARBS, 9 G PROTEIN

BECAUSE OF THE PROTEIN-PACKED QUINOA, THIS DISH ALSO MAKES A DELICIOUS, FILLING, VEGETARIAN MAIN DISH.

BAKED PARMESAN SWEET POTATO TOTS

Instead of deep-frying white potatoes for standard tots, I baked up a flavorful sweet potato mixture. Sweet potatoes are one of nature's greatest sources of vitamin A and by baking instead of frying them, the tots get crunchy and tasty without the added fat and calories of oil.

MAKES: 4 servings
TIME: 40 minutes

Cooking spray

1 large sweet potato, peeled and shredded finely

1 large egg

1 cup whole wheat panko bread crumbs, divided

⅓ cup grated Parmesan cheese

Preheat the oven to 350°F. Spray a baking sheet with cooking spray; set aside. In a mixing bowl, combine the sweet potato, egg, ½ cup of the bread crumbs, and the Parmesan. On a plate, spread out the remaining ½ cup of bread crumbs in a thin layer. Using clean hands, form the sweet potato mixture into small tot shapes. Roll in the bread crumbs and place on the prepared baking sheet. Spray the tops of the tots with cooking spray. Bake for 30 to 35 minutes, or until browned and crunchy.

NUTRITION PER SERVING: 206 CALORIES, 5.7 G FAT, 29.0 G CARBS, 11.7 G PROTEIN

SERVE THESE TOTS WITH LOTS OF KETCHUP FOR DIPPING!

HEIRLOOM TOMATO FLATBREAD

This is, hands down, my favorite dinner of summer. Not only is it ready in 20 minutes, but it also has so much explosive flavor that you can only get from ripe tomatoes and herbs during summertime.

MAKES: *4 servings*
TIME: *20 minutes*

1 loaf ciabatta bread, sliced horizontally to make two long, flat loaves

¼ cup olive oil, divided

2 cloves garlic

4 to 6 ripe tomatoes, sliced thinly

Handful of fresh herbs, minced (I used basil, oregano, and parsley)

Salt and pepper

Preheat the grill to high heat. Using a pastry brush, brush 1 tablespoon of the olive oil over the cut side of each half of the ciabatta bread. Place the bread, cut side down, on the grill grate and grill until browned and toasted, about 5 minutes, flip the bread, and grill for an additional 5 minutes. Remove from the grill. Rub the garlic clove over the cut side of the toasted bread, then layer the bread with tomato slices, sprinkle with herbs, drizzle with the remaining olive oil, and season with salt and pepper to taste. Place back on the grill, close the lid, and grill just to heat through, about 5 minutes. Remove from the grill and season with salt and pepper to taste.

NUTRITION PER SERVING: 326 CALORIES, 16.1 G FAT, 42.1 G CARBS, 7.1 G PROTEIN

CUT THESE FLATBREADS INTO SMALLER PIECES TO MAKE A GREAT, EASY APPETIZER FOR YOUR SUMMER COOKOUTS.

TOMATOES

Tomatoes are definitely one of the staple produce items in most households. Even those people who can't stomach raw tomatoes still seem to find a spot on their menu for tomato sauces and tomato-based dishes. It's a good thing tomatoes are so pervasive, because their superfood status makes them worthy of your dinner table.

QUICK FACTS

1 Tomatoes are an excellent source of lycopene, an important antioxidant in the fight against cancer and cardiovascular disease.

2 Tomatoes come in a wide variety of colors, shapes, sizes, and styles.

HEALTH BENEFITS

Lycopene, lycopene, lycopene! Tomatoes are packed with the antioxidant lycopene, which has been proven to help maintain bone and cardiovascular health, and help prevent cancer. While much of the purported benefits of lycopene have been related to men's health issues (specific-ally, helping to prevent prostate cancer), new research is indicating that lycopene is just as important in women's diets as well—numerous studies have shown a reduction in the risk of breast cancer and cardiovascular disease in women who consume sufficient amounts of lycopene.

AVAILABILITY

Tomatoes are available year-round in most supermarkets, but they are one produce item that really should be avoided during the off-season. Not only are they lacking in flavor and texture in the winter months, but they're missing the nutrients of their vine-ripened, in-season summer versions. Pick up fresh tomatoes at your local farmers' market or farm stand in the summer and really enjoy the flavor and health benefits of summer tomatoes!

In the past, the thought has been that the more red the fruit or veggie, the higher the lycopene, but recent studies are showing that all colors, shapes, and varieties of tomatoes have lycopene. In fact, depending on the color, the tomato may contain a slightly different version of lycopene. So stock up on red, yellow, orange, purple, pink, black, and white tomatoes!

HOW TO USE

Eating them raw is a great way to get the full nutrient potential of tomatoes, but you can also use tomatoes as a base for salads, salsa, sauces, and more.

NUTRITION HIGHLIGHTS PER 1 MEDIUM-SIZE TOMATO

26	0.4g	5.7g	1g	20%	15%	273.1mg
CALORIES	FAT	CARBS	PROTEIN	VITAMIN C	VITAMIN A	POTASSIUM

WALNUTS

Recent studies have shown that only a small percentage of adults eat raw tree nuts regularly. That's a shame! Tree nuts, such as walnuts, are packed with vitamins, minerals, antioxidants, and healthy fats and protein.

QUICK FACTS

1 Walnuts are packed with compounds that prevent cardiovascular disease.

2 The antioxidants and anti-inflammatories in walnuts also work as anticancer agents.

3 Walnuts may help balance blood sugar in type 2 diabetics.

HEALTH BENEFITS

Walnuts have a lot of benefits to our body, but none as well documented as their cardiovascular benefits. A diet rich in walnuts has been shown to decrease "bad" cholesterol, overall cholesterol, and the risk of excessive clotting, and help regulate blood pressure. Healthy hearts thrive on walnuts!

Packed with a wide variety of antioxidants and anti-inflammatory compounds, walnuts are also showing promising benefits in fighting cancer and treating type 2 diabetes.

AVAILABILITY

You can find walnuts at most grocery stores. For the best nutrition, do not remove the flaky skin from shelled walnuts—researchers believe nearly 90 percent of the flavonoids are located in that skin.

Walnuts also grow well in the majority of North America, so keep an eye out for local walnuts at your farmers' market.

HOW TO USE

Because walnuts are high in fat, they are perishable and best kept in the fridge or freezer. Eat walnuts raw, chop them and add them to yogurt or cereal, or put them in baked goods.

BASIL-WALNUT PESTO

Standard pesto is made with pine nuts, which is fine, but pine nuts can be pretty costly and don't offer nearly the awesome healthy benefits of walnuts. Walnuts are readily available, and have a similar taste and texture to pine nuts—you won't notice the difference.

MAKES: 1 cup pesto
TIME: 10 minutes

2 cups packed basil leaves

½ cup walnuts, toasted

2 cloves garlic

½ cup shredded Parmesan cheese

½ teaspoon salt

⅓ to ½ cup extra-virgin olive oil

Combine all the ingredients in a food processor. Pulse until smooth, adding more olive oil if necessary to thin.

NUTRITION PER TABLESPOON:
72 CALORIES, 7.2 G FAT, 0.7 G CARBS,
2.0 G PROTEIN

IT'S HARD TO BEAT A SPOONFUL OF FRESH PESTO MIXED WITH HOT PASTA—IT'S A QUICK, EASY, AND SUPER YUMMY DINNER!

CHIA WATERMELON AGUA FRESCA

Aguas frescas are a commonplace refreshing drink in much of Mexico and Latin America. They're usually a combination of water, fresh fruit, and a touch of sweetener. This drink is incredibly hydrating, thanks to a hefty dose of chia seeds. The chia seeds absorb the liquid and form a gel that is fun to drink and helps hydrate your digestive tract.

MAKES: 1 serving
TIME: 5 minutes

2 cups cubed seedless watermelon

½ cup water

1 tablespoon honey

1 tablespoon lime juice

2 tablespoons chia seeds

In a blender, combine the watermelon, water, honey, and lime juice. Blend on high speed until smooth. Add the chia seeds and pulse until mixed. Let the drink rest for 5 minutes before drinking.

NUTRITION PER SERVING: 155 CALORIES, 0.5 G FAT, 40.2 G CARBS, 1.9 G PROTEIN

LEARN ALL ABOUT THE AWESOME HEALTH BENEFITS OF CHIA SEEDS ON PAGE 200.

WATERMELON, FETA & BASIL BITES

The combination of salty cheese, an earthy herb, and delectably sweet melon might seem strange, but it's a real crowd-pleaser. And while these appetizers look fancy when displayed on a pretty white platter, they take about five minutes to pull together—perfect for a quick and easy starter for your summer dinner party.

MAKES: *12 bites*
TIME: *5 minutes*

¼ cup balsamic vinegar

24 bite-size watermelon chunks (seedless preferred)

12 fresh basil leaves

5 ounces feta, cut into 12 bite-size pieces

Bring the balsamic vinegar to a boil in a small saucepan over medium-high heat. Lower the heat and simmer until thickened, about 2 minutes. Assemble the bites by placing one watermelon chunk on a toothpick, followed by a basil leaf and a piece of feta, and topped with another watermelon chunk. Repeat with remaining ingredients. Drizzle with the reduced balsamic vinegar right before serving.

NUTRITION PER BITE: 69 CALORIES, 2.7 G FAT, 9.8 G CARBS, 9.8 G PROTEIN

IF YOU PREFER, YOU CAN USE A MELON BALLER TO MAKE NEAT LITTLE WATERMELON BALLS FOR THE BITES.

Many Thanks

To the team at The Countryman Press and W. W. Norton, thank you for opening your arms wide and accepting me into your creative, supportive, and amazing family. Working with you has been one of the most fulfilling and exciting seasons of my life, and I'm so excited to keep producing more yumminess with you!

To my blog readers, friends, and sponsors, none of this would have been possible without your love, support, and encouragement. It's incredible to me that a little blog that started with no one reading it five years ago has blossomed into a brand-new career in food writing for me. And all of that is thanks to each and every person who ever clicked on one of my recipes. Thanks.

To my family and friends, having the kind of support network I do is what gave me the confidence to take the leap and make this whole recipe development thing my career. Thank you for never questioning my crazy plans or ideas (well, at least in front of me). And thank you for all the love and support that help me get through every day.

To my husband, thank you for not batting an eyelash when I tell you we're having beet burgers or freekeh "meat" balls for dinner. In fact, thank you for showing excitement, interest, and pride in every single creation I make. You could never know how important that kind of support is to my creative process. I wouldn't be the person I am today without you and your undying support.

To my JuneBug, you are my reason for everything, little girl. You make me want to be the best version of myself. And that is the best gift anyone could give me. Thank you.

About the Author

By day, Cassie Johnston works as a graphic designer, but after hours, Cassie is obsessed with all things edible. This love of growing, cooking, and eating food, led to a second career in food writing, photography, and recipe development.

Cassie is a champion for local and organic food and, along with her husband and daughter, runs a small hobby farm in southern Indiana producing heirloom vegetables, cut flowers, and maple syrup. Cassie shares her passion for cooking and eating daily at her healthy recipe blog, *Back to Her Roots* (backtoherroots.com).

When Cassie isn't writing about veggies, you can find her hiking through the beautiful Indiana countryside, enjoying craft beer and daydreaming about next year's crops.

Index